Praise for *The Smart Veggie Patch*

'*The Smart Veggie Patch* is a razor sharp call to action, clearly laying out the importance and need to take a personal stake in growing your own food. Rather than treading an esoteric path of whimsy, Terry details how judicious use of technology and design can empower us to take a firm grasp, not only on the food we eat, but on our health, the health of those we love and the health of the planet.'

Paul West, bestselling cookbook and gardening writer

'An inspirational read from someone who walks the talk. Terry shares his family's garden journey with passion, honesty, and a wealth of lived experience. The lessons and clearly articulated reasoning in this book will give you the why, and the how, of growing your own.'

Christina Giudici, co-founder of FIMBY – Food In My Back Yard

'In a concise, easy to read volume, Terry Memory gives a powerful reminder of why we should all try to grow our own food, along with all the practical knowhow to achieve just that.'

Matthew Evans and Sadie Chrestman

As a passionate advocate for holistic health, sustainability and personal responsibility, Terry Memory offers a unique perspective and practical solutions to how we can best create a food system for the future.

Terry, his wife Gemma and their six children live on a sustainable organic farm in the forest-clad hills of the Huon Valley in southern Tasmania. Over the last decade, he has gained firsthand knowledge of what it takes to live truly sustainably and how to radically improve our health with the food we eat. This journey, while fraught with numerous trials and errors, culminated in the creation of the Smart Garden concept and the Technograrian approach to homegrown food production.

Terry is also a highly successful health food entrepreneur. He and Gemma founded the 13 Seeds Hemp Farm on their kitchen table in 2016. The company saw them develop Australia's largest range of award-winning Hemp Food and Skincare products, including several Australian firsts. This led them to become one of the first businesses to process hemp seed in Australia, and they also created Tasmania's first Hemp Food manufacturing facility. In 2021, the company was listed on the Australian stock exchange and now has tens of thousands of happy and loyal customers.

The combination of pragmatic hands-on experience, personal insight into industrial food production and tireless research into the realities of and potential solutions for our current food system form the basis of this book.

THE SMART VEGGIE PATCH

TERRY MEMORY

Pan Macmillan Australia

Pan Macmillan acknowledges the Traditional Custodians of country throughout Australia and their connections to lands, waters and communities. We pay our respect to Elders past and present and extend that respect to all Aboriginal and Torres Strait Islander peoples today. We honour more than sixty thousand years of storytelling, art and culture.

First published 2022 in Macmillan by Pan Macmillan Australia Pty Ltd
1 Market Street, Sydney, New South Wales, Australia, 2000

A catalogue record for this book is available from the National Library of Australia

Typeset in Baskerville by Midland Typesetters, Australia

Printed by IVE

We advise that the information contained in this book does not negate personal responsibility on the part of the reader for their own health and safety. It is recommended that individually tailored advice is sought from your healthcare or medical professional. The publishers and their respective employees, agents and authors, are not liable for injuries or damage occasioned to any person as a result of reading or following the information contained in this book.

The author and the publisher have made every effort to contact copyright holders for material used in this book. Any person or organisation that may have been overlooked should contact the publisher.

Cover image/s used for illustrative purposes only

The paper in this book is FSC® certified.
FSC® promotes environmentally responsible, socially beneficial and economically viable management of the world's forests.

This book is dedicated to the seven parts of me.

For my eldest sons, Isaac and Joshua, who are the legs that drive me strongly forward with hope. For my eldest daughters, Anna and Lucy, who are the arms that I lovingly embrace the world with. For the little two, Samuel and Emily, who are the eyes with which I see the true beauty and wonder of life.

For my extraordinary wife, Gemma, who is the heart that beats within me and whose soul I gratefully share.

I am blessed.

CONTENTS

'Odd as I am sure it will appear to some, I can think of no better form of personal involvement in the cure of the environment than that of gardening. A person who is growing a garden, if he is growing it organically, is improving a piece of the world. He is producing something to eat, which makes him somewhat independent of the grocery business, but he is also enlarging, for himself, the meaning of food and the pleasure of eating.'

– Wendell Berry, author, environmental activist and small-scale farmer, and a voice for the benefits of local small-scale agriculture as a way to heal many of our current societal issues

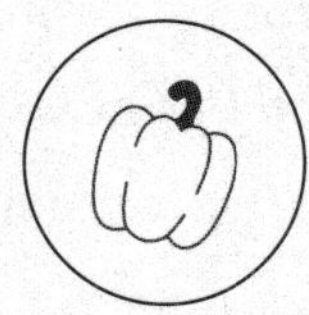

INTRODUCTION

'We're only truly secure when we can look out our kitchen window and see our food growing and our friends working nearby.'

– Bill Mollison, researcher, author, scientist, teacher and biologist, considered by many to be the father of permaculture

Our food, the sources from which it is derived and its ability to promote positive health outcomes have been long-held passions for my wife and myself. It is a passion that stems from our desire to be moral human beings, wanting to be healthy and get the most out of life. Of equal importance is our need, as parents, to provide our children with the most nutritious start in life we can. As our eldest child is now an adult, this passion has consumed more than 20 years of our lives. We have endeavoured to raise our six children as healthily and happily as possible. It has driven our compulsion to dig deeper and thoroughly research the truth behind the food we provide for them; to question, research, assess, plan and act.

This need to act led us to become the founders of health-related businesses in the consumer food space, including one of Australia's largest hemp-based food and skincare companies. Managing these businesses showed us firsthand how diet and what we put into and onto our bodies are critical for our health, happiness and a life long-lived. It taught us the essential elements of achieving positive outcomes for our holistic wellbeing through our food. It also revealed how seemingly innocuous food business activities generate vast unintentional adverse health and environmental consequences.

Perhaps the most significant factor that set us on our Smart Garden journey was the reality check we received when faced with a life-threatening environmental disaster. We lived in the small country town of Warburton in Victoria, Australia. This picturesque village on Melbourne's outskirts formed part of a tourist route that included the Kingslake and Marysville townships. As it is now known, the Black Saturday bushfires of 2009 killed 173 people. It destroyed both the townships of Kingslake and Marysville.

The fire caught us by surprise. Despite living in one of the most bushfire-prone areas globally, we found ourselves desperately unprepared and ill-equipped. We had fallen under the delusion that our safety was somehow someone else's concern. We had never experienced a bushfire of this magnitude before. As such, we did not appreciate the real and present threat it posed. As the sky glowed red, burning embers fell all around us, and disbelief and fear suffocated our decision-making ability. Some level of forethought and pre-planning would have saved us from living through the horror of realising that we may have decided to leave too late. And we could have avoided the panic and fear our children saw in our eyes at that moment if we had better appreciated and understood the situation in which we found ourselves.

In the months after the fire, we tried to grapple with the what-ifs of that horrible day. We knew our inaction and lack of pre-planning or preparation had placed our children and us in serious jeopardy. We made the sobering discovery that somehow, in the atrophying malaise that is Western living, we had ceded our personal responsibility by our reliance on public safety institutions. Installed in us was a lifetime of programming that told us that help is always on the way. The haunting realisation we now knew to be true was that sometimes 'help' is somewhere else trying to save their own families. Sometimes that 'help' is just too overwhelmed, and sometimes that 'help' just cannot do anything to help you. Ultimately, you have to be able to help yourself!

After that fateful day, Gemma and I made a pact. Our family's essential needs and safety were now our responsibility. We would never again be 100 per cent reliant on anyone or anything to take care of our family . . . and so our Smart Garden journey began.

As a society, the way we currently provide food for ourselves and our families has profoundly disconnected us from what is an acutely necessary, natural process, and from many of the vital benefits the process provides for our human experience. This disconnectedness is a by-product of an industrialised food system. Society now values convenience far more than connection. The consequences of this disconnection from how our food is grown, produced and consumed are numerous. Rising chronic disease rates, environmental devastation and endemic social inequality are all symptoms.

With this book, I wanted to take a hard look at the future of food in relation to what we eat and our health, how we currently procure our food and how we can best manage the inevitable risks of our uncertain future. I wanted to lift the veil on just what our industrialised food system really costs us and how it simply cannot and will not continue in its current form. I wanted to consider and compare the economic costs and environmental, health and social costs as well. While the present realities are outlined, it is the systemic risk our current food system poses to global disruption and its potential collapse in the future that is perhaps most concerning.

We are confronted with myriad economic, environmental, health and social crises and issues via the media, governmental bodies or concerned activists. Unsurprisingly, our current industrialised food system is a significant contributor to all of these extensive problems. We need to remove our tacit involvement in and reliance upon it to move towards a healthier society and world.

With the rise in chronic diet-related disease and illness, we can no longer fool ourselves into believing that much of the food we purchase is good for us. Global medical records and data confirm the opposite. As our health is a crucial pillar in the enjoyment of life and billions of dollars are spent every year on health kicks and regimes, how can we be getting more malnourished and obese at the same time? The food we consume is the fuel that drives our health outcomes. We are only beginning to really understand the complicated relationship between our food and our bodies.

Our current food system makes us chronically sick and catastrophically destroys our planet and its ecosystems. Almost every aspect of the industrialised food system carries with it unacceptable levels of negative consequences and outcomes – from the destruction of arable land and our oceans and the poisoning and contamination of our waterways and environments, to the economic impoverishment of people and countries and the abject cruelty and death inflicted on millions of animals every single day.

The future food security for ourselves and our families is paramount. To quote an old African proverb, 'You cannot tell a hungry child you gave him food yesterday.' Our reliance on the current food system puts us all at significant risk when, inevitably, the system begins to falter and break down. I hope this book will show you our current system's perilous situation and how many people are already planning for a vastly different food future.

We have all recently seen how the COVID-19 outbreak has impacted food supply chains and caused empty grocery shelves and out-of-stock items. Many of us do not know that we also faced a massive food shortage in 2007–08 that was only just averted from becoming a major global crisis. This shortage saw food-related riots occur in more than 30 countries[1] with very little associated media coverage. Several factors were the catalyst for the dramatic rise in the cost of staple food commodities like wheat and rice, where prices almost doubled. These factors include but are not limited to reduced agricultural output, climate change effects and mismanagement by the global governance that controls the vast majority of food production and distribution.[2]

In the near future, we will be required to be much more personally responsible for creating and supplying our most basic needs. As global populations continue to grow, the cost of energy-related infrastructure for bankrupt governments will become too great. Even as I write this, California, one of the world's most advanced populated areas, suffers from rolling blackouts due to summer electricity shortages. The creation of energy is a necessity for life. As we can now create the energy for our homes in the form of electricity from solar, we will also need to create calorific energy for our bodies via growing our own food.

There is a simple homegrown way you can permanently access tasty and highly nutritious food while dramatically reducing your reliance on a broken and destructive system. The solution has been part of our daily human lives from the beginning of our agrarian-based existence thousands of years ago. Thankfully now, with science and modern technology, it is far easier, cheaper and more beneficial than our forebears could have dreamed.

As the science and technology of creating electrical energy within our homes have advanced dramatically over the last 20 years, so have the science and technology around creating food with home gardens. Gemma and I have incorporated these advances into our garden to create what we believe could be more accurately called a 'food production system'. It is a system that makes successfully producing food a lot easier to manage, far healthier and much more bountiful than a typical home vegetable garden. Over the last ten years, we have adopted, revised and redesigned the system – we call it our Smart Garden.

With this book, I will show you how modern science, technology and a greater understanding of the incredibly complex natural processes that interplay in a home garden can vastly increase your success rates. You'll discover how technology and automation can radically reduce the labour, time and knowledge you personally require to enjoy an utterly amazing and bountiful Smart Garden. I will also discuss why there is an urgent need to futureproof your family's food security and how our current industrialised food supply is making us sicker, destroying the environment and creating massive inequality in the world. We will look at some of the shocking realities of global food supply and, more positively and significantly, how a homegrown food production system can make a real difference. I will show you how it will not only improve your health and well-being but how it is also a profoundly proactive step in reducing your impact on the Earth.

This book is filled with the things we have learned over the last decade. I will share how to create your Smart Garden and the basic things you will need to consider with its design and building, and how to get the most from it with the least cost and effort. We currently grow 70–80 per cent of our food requirements from our Smart Garden for ourselves and our six children. I will outline the plan you need to provide yourself and your family with the absolute best nutrient- and mineral-rich, health-giving food. You'll also learn how you can create a secondary stream of income and a bartering commodity with your produce. I will show you how you can ensure that you and your family have enough food for whatever the future holds. You can have peace of mind knowing that you have guaranteed that your loved ones will never have to go hungry.

Ultimately, we have to urgently change the way we produce and consume food if we are to save ourselves, the planet and the future. I hope this book provides you with the inspiration and urgency to begin your journey to creating your very own Smart Garden today.

PART ONE

WHAT OUR FOOD REALLY COSTS US

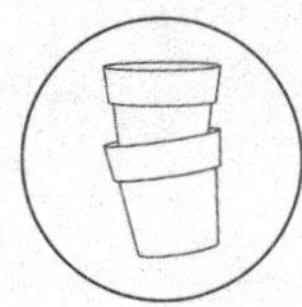

THE HIDDEN COSTS OF THE FOOD INDUSTRY

'The cost of a thing is the amount of what I will call life which is required to be exchanged for it, immediately or in the long run.'

– Henry David Thoreau, naturalist, essayist and practical philosopher whose best-known work, *Walden*, was a contemplation on living simply in natural surroundings

As part of writing this book, I felt it would be essential to know just how much the current globalised food system is costing us as consumers. I wanted to weigh up the cost of setting up and maintaining a Smart Garden versus the cost of our current consumer habits. I can quickly produce accurate figures for what a Smart Garden might cost. Those costs are relatively fixed and finite. It proved vastly more challenging to find and calculate the cost of our globalised industrial food system. That, in comparison, is anything but fixed and finite.

As we line up at our local supermarket, the checkout operator scans the prices of our selected grocery items. We get to see, for a second, the retail price of each item flash up on the cash register screen. From my experience in business, I know many different factors can determine a retail product price. In its simplest terms, companies calculate what it has cost them to create, build and distribute the product and then add a profit margin to it. Those two figures are then added together to produce the retail price. That is the price we pay as consumers.

Or is it?

This retail price does not take into account many other negative costs in its calculation. Why? Because companies do not have to pay for, nor are they held responsible for, these costs. They never appear on a company's financial report or shareholders' statement, even though they happen due to the company's operations. These additional negative costs are like collateral damage during wartime. They are the consequences of the company's mission to create profits from the need to feed the world.

So who pays for them? We all do.

Publicly available information on the additional negative costs of our current food system is minimal. The data that I could find are estimates, approximations or best guesses. The issue is incredibly complex. How do we put a cost on environmental destruction? How do we measure the greenhouse gas emissions of the global food transport industry? How do we calculate the diet-related health costs across multiple countries and currencies?

To highlight this lack of accurate data, it is worth noting that no one actually knows what the globalised food system is worth in dollar terms. Best guesstimates would appear to be between US$5–8 trillion. When the Food and Agriculture Organization (FAO) of the United Nations calculates the cost of greenhouse gas emissions from deforestation related to wasted food production, the costs are estimated to range between US$10 billion and US$350 billion per year. That is a vast variation as to what the actual cost might be. While the lack of hard empirical data makes any review problematic, I believe the following will help us better understand the true scale of these additional negative costs.

Let us look at the data as it stands on what our food is *really* costing us.

These are some of the negative cost realities of our estimated US$8 trillion global food system:

- **Environmental Costs** – Cost associated with the destruction of the environment via the food production/consumption cycle, e.g. pollution of air, land and water, deforestation, plastic waste, chemicals, methane emissions.
- **Social Costs** – Costs of the destruction of the relationships and proper function of societies and communities, e.g. wellbeing loss, risk of conflict, acute health effects of pesticides.
- **Economic Costs** – Negative costs associated with the entire food production/consumption cycle, e.g. food wastage, health-care, food aid, loss of productivity.
- **Health Costs** – Costs associated with the negative health impacts through diet-related illness and disease, e.g. malnutrition, obesity, diet-related chronic diseases.
- **Farm Subsidy Costs** – Cost to taxpayers supporting farm-based agricultural businesses, e.g. income support payments, grants and loans.

ENVIRONMENTAL COSTS

This cost refers to what we pay in environmental factors or natural capital to produce the food we eat. Natural capital refers to the

Earth's assets or resources of air, water, land and all living things. Most of these resources have taken millennia to form and build to the abundance we once enjoyed. Currently, the natural capital cost of our food production system is grossly underestimated if not wholly ignored. The destruction of natural capital also includes many other aspects associated with environmental pollution, greenhouse gas emissions, and the loss of native animals and insects.

Unlike financial capital that must be accounted for, corporations can monetise the use of our global natural capital for their financial gain. Putting a price on the impact of these costs is difficult. How could the destruction of the Amazon rainforest be accurately measured? Whatever cost current researchers place on an acre of virgin Amazonian rainforest will undoubtedly be far less than that of future generations.

SOCIAL COSTS

Social capital is defined as the network of relationships of people who live and work in a particular society, enabling that society to function properly. Social capital is our connection to each other. It is easy to see when the social capital of a society has been affected by events like famine, forest destruction and land contamination. Populations become isolated and are often forced to leave their land and homes to find safer refuge. Destruction of social capital leads to the complete collapse of society. Many societies are unable to ever re-establish the pre-event level of social capital they once enjoyed.

Consider the impact of famine from the desertification of land from commercial overgrazing and crop production. Populations from developing nations face malnutrition, starvation and often death when commercial agricultural practices go unchecked in marginal areas. These types of events destroy the social capital of the communities and societies that are affected. The damage caused to this vital social capital never appears on a company's balance sheet. It is a by-product of rampant natural capital destruction for corporate gain.

Like the Amazonian rainforest issue I touched on earlier, how do you arrive at a cost figure representing the value of community or human life? We should all hope that whatever value we do place on them increases as our compassion and understanding hopefully improve in the future.

ECONOMIC COSTS

These are the costs associated with the destruction of economies that are a by-product of our globalised food production system. Around the world, and in particular for developing countries, the destruction of natural and social capital for food production leads to crippling economic conditions. Often the economic cost is simply caused by inequitable global food distribution. If populations are malnourished due to food shortages, they are far less able to be economically productive.

Again, very few companies or corporations are held accountable for the economic damage they inflict in the operation of their business. Suppose any financial reparations are offered or paid. In that case, they will usually find their way into the pockets of a limited few. The ways and means by which our food is currently produced does impact regional economies around the world. This again must be considered if we are to recognise the true costs of what we purchase and consume.

Food wastage is also part of the economic cost of our food system. The one-third of global food production that is wasted immediately adds 33 per cent to the cost of the food that is consumed. Additionally, it also means that the wasted portion cannot be used to feed the world's hungry.

On the following page is a chart of figures from research by the FAO from 2014.[3] They produced a full cost accounting report on global food wastage and found that one-third of all the food the world produces is never eaten. It is lost, wasted or just not consumed. Interestingly, poorer countries waste the most food during production, and richer countries waste the most at the point of consumption. The report considered all costs associated with producing this wasted portion of global food production. The cost of factors like greenhouse gas emissions, soil contamination, water pollution, health effects of pesticides and livelihood loss were all included.

In total, the report included 24 different costs that are directly attributed to the production of our food. I used the figures from this chart to calculate the possible environmental, social and economic costs of our current food system.

What struck me in the research is that while the report focuses on the costs related to the wasted proportion of food production, these costs must also be relative to the portion we do consume. I have used these costs as recognised by the UN and extrapolated to include the entire global food system of wasted and consumed food.

HEALTH COSTS

The health costs associated with the food we eat are truly staggering and very hard to quantify. As countries can significantly differ in their consumption preferences and patterns, it is not accurate to simply extrapolate a few countries' health costs when calculating the

Estimated Cost of Food Wastage (in USD)

Atmosphere

Greenhouse gas emissions
(without deforestation/organic soils)
GHG from deforestation
GHG from managed organic soils
Ammonia emissions

Estimated Cost
$395 billion

Cost Range
$5–1941 billion

Water

Pesticides in drinking water
Nitrates in drinking water
Pollution Nitrate eutrophication
Pollution Phosphorus eutrophication
Water use (Irrigation only)
Water scarcity

Estimated Cost
$196 billion

Cost Range
$192–205 billion

Soil

Erosion (water)
Erosion (wind/uncertain)
Land occupation (deforestation)

Estimated Cost
$73 billion

Cost Range
$17–143 billion

Biodiversity

Impacts of pesticide use
Impacts of nitrate eutrophication
Impacts of phosphorus eutrophication
Pollinator losses
Fisheries overexploitation

Estimated Cost
$32 billion

Cost Range
$18–42 billion

Social

Livelihood loss
Health damages (wellbeing loss)
Acute health effects of pesticides
Risk of conflict

Estimated Cost
$882 billion

Economic

Value of products lost and wasted
Agricultural subsidies
(OECD Only)

Estimated Cost
$1055 billion

Sub-total environmental costs = $696 billion
Sub-total social costs = $882 billion
Sub-total economic costs = $1055 billion
TOTAL COST (all categories) = $2633 billion

global cost burden of diet-related chronic disease. For example, in the US, it is estimated that the direct medical and loss of productivity costs of diet-related chronic disease exceed US$1 trillion. As the US represents only 4.25 per cent of the global population, that would amount to a global health cost figure of more than US$23 trillion, or almost 20 per cent of global GDP!

As we know, diet-related chronic disease is particularly prevalent in wealthier economies. Still, we must also consider the diet-related health costs of malnutrition, starvation and death that affect the world's poor. This, too, is an endemic part of our current globalised food system. Inequitable food distribution, the use of quality crops as stock feed, and food insecurity are just a few of the underlying issues. Today, more than 820 million people in the world do not have enough to eat. This staggering fact is both a health and a humanitarian crisis.

I have used the following chart from Martin Van Neiuwkop, the Director of Agricultural Global Practice at the World Bank, to calculate the potential global health cost of malnutrition and obesity. These figures are broad ranging and do not consider a host of other diet-related health issues that are not associated with malnutrition or obesity.

In 2019, the National Heart, Lung and Blood Institute in the US put the price tag on the impact of America's poor diets on cardiometabolic diseases such as heart disease, stroke and type 2 diabetes at $50 billion annually.[4] Let's look at the top five diet-related chronic diseases and take estimated cost figures from the leading foundations, associations and societies dedicated to each particular disease. We find that the US alone is spending more than a trillion dollars a year combating these diseases.

Food System Problem	**Annual Economic Costs ($ trillions)**
2 billion people under- and malnourished (3 percent 2018 global GDP)	2.43
2 billion people overweight and obese (2 percent of 2018 global GDP)	1.62
One third of agriculture production lost or wasted	1.07
Economic loss due to insufficient food safety	0.11
Economic loss due to land use and land cover change in terrestrial ecosystems (0.41 percent of 2018 global GDP)	0.33
25 percent of land degraded due to poor management practices (0.25 percent of 2018 global GDP)	0.20
13 percent global emissions from agriculture, other than from land use change (49.1 GT CO2 at $ 40/ton)	0.27
Costs still to be accounted for	
Biodiversity loss other than losses due to land use change (e.g., loss of pollination services, degraded wetlands, etc.)	
Health costs due to chemical and pesticide use, including from deteriorating water quality	
Contribution to rising anti-microbial resistance and associated costs	
Total costs	***6.03***

I have used these figures as a guide to the costs of global malnutrition and obesity as a basis for the potential health costs.

Disease	**Data**	**Source**	**Cost**
Cardiovascular and stroke	2016	American Heart Association	US$320.1 billion
Cancer	2009	American Cancer Society	US$216.6 billion
Diabetes	2017	American Diabetes Association	US$327 billion
Obesity	2017	United Health Foundation	US$342.2 billion
Osteoporosis	2016	National Osteoporosis Foundation	US$19 billion
Total cost: US$1.224 trillion			

While we cannot generalise the US figures because of the varied and unique diets and health situations we find worldwide, we can use this figure as a potential guide. Given that the US population represents less than 5 per cent of the global population, we can see that the diet-related global health cost worldwide would be staggering.

FARM SUBSIDY COSTS

Another significant part of the economic cost of our food production is by way of government subsidies. Many governments around the world use taxpayer revenue to prop up food production enterprises. These subsidies can be used to inflate commodity prices and often create artificial minimum price levels. The effectiveness of subsidies to provide these outcomes is contentious. The sums received often dramatically outweigh any benefits they provide. Currently, we spend more than US$2 billion per day ($730 billion annually) in global farm subsidies. This must be included when we consider that the subsidies' cost amounts to 12 per cent of all the revenue the farming industry generates.

Total Estimated Agricultural Supports (subsidies) in 2019

These totals are ranked as the amount spent in relation to the gross amount earned from agriculuture in each country.

1. Norway	**$3.03 billion**	**57.6%**
2. Iceland	**$223.2 million**	**54.6%**
3. Switzerland	**$6.16 billion**	**47.4%**
4. Korea	**$20.8 billion**	**46.1%**
5. Japan	**$37.6 billion**	**41.3%**
6. Phillipines	**$7.3 billion**	**27.1%**
7. Indonesia	**$29.4 billion**	**23.3%**
8. European Union	**$101.3 billion**	**19.0%**
9. Israel	**$1.5 billion**	**17.4%**
10. Turkey	**$6.7 billion**	**13.5%**

These totals are ranked by total spend on agricultural subsides

1. China	**$185.9 billion**	**12.1%**
2. European Union	**$101.3 billion**	**19.0%**
3. United States	**$48.9 billion**	**12.1%**
4. Japan	**$37.6 billion**	**41.3%**
5. Indonesia	**$29.4 billion**	**23.3%**
6. Korea	**$20.8 billion**	**46.1%**
7. Russia	**$7.9 billion**	**9.2%**
8. Phillipines	**$7.3 billion**	**27.1%**
9. Turkey	**$6.7 billion**	**13.5%**
10. Switzerland	**$6.2 billion**	**47.4%**

Many of the costs I have listed above are interrelated. The destruction of natural capital is directly linked to the destruction of social capital, and economic costs directly relate to health costs. Suppose we were to make more informed decisions around what we eat and take responsibility for the actual costs inherent in every shopping trolley. In that case, we would need new metrics included in those decisions. Perhaps product labels should show how much a product contributed to these negative consequences. Like the nutrition information that already appears on our food products, these metrics would help us make far more informed decisions about what we are genuinely willing to pay. Unfortunately, without all of us being far more aware of the reality of our current food system, the ultimate price will be paid by future generations.

To get a better picture of what these additional costs would add to every dollar we spend at a supermarket and in relation to an average weekly Australian grocery shop, I have used some simple tables below.

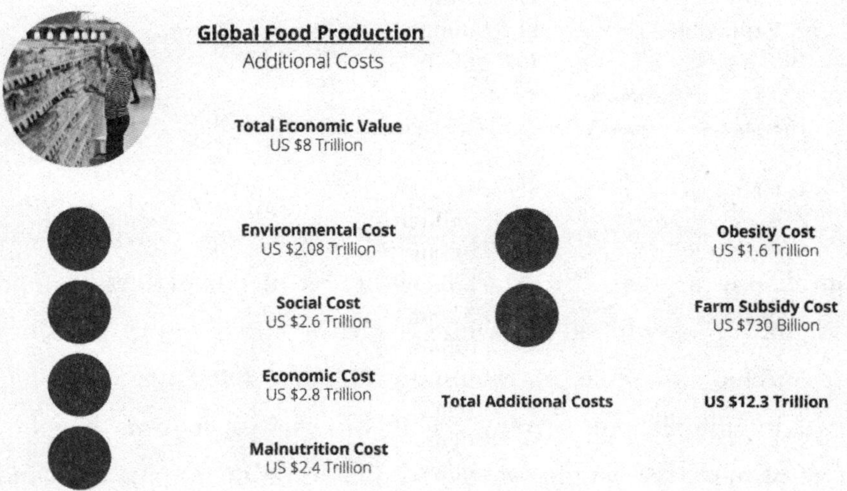

For every $1 spent		Source
Environmental Cost	**$0.26**	*FAO
Social Cost	**$0.33**	*FAO
Economic Cost	**$0.35**	*FAO
Malnutrition Cost	**$0.30**	*World Bank
Obesity Cost	**$0.20**	*World Bank
Global Farm Subsidies	**$0.09**	*OECD
Total added costs	**$1.53**	

For an average Australian household shopping bill of $236.97*, we are actually paying another **$364.93** in environmental, social, economic and health-related costs.

For an average $236.97* grocery shop		Source
Environmental Cost	**$61.85**	*FAO
Social Cost	**$78.38**	*FAO
Economic Cost	**$83.18**	*FAO
Malnutrition Cost	**$71.98**	*World Bank
Obesity Cost	**$47.92**	*World Bank
Global Farm Subsidies	**$21.62**	*OECD
Total added costs	**$364.93**	

- $236.97 - Based on Australian Bureau of Statistics Data 2015
- Figures are not exchange rate weighted

With these estimations, we are trying to place a cost or dollar value on all the negative consequences inherent in our globalised food system. It is easy to see that with every shopping trolley of groceries we purchase, there are many considerable negative costs.

Undoubtedly our current system brings with it some benefits. The primary one would be that we play little or no part in it and take little or no responsibility for it. For that, we are willing to pay an ever-increasing price. It is also extremely convenient to know that whatever you need will be sitting on a shelf and available to you at all times. The removal of the responsibility for creating and producing our food and 24-hour, 7-day-a-week shopping convenience are the cornerstones of current food consumerism.

Although we have become so endemically reliant on the current industrialised food system, we must acknowledge its unacceptable costs. If we are to proffer some responsible level of decision-making for our collective futures, these other costs must become part of a new, conscious consumerism. Separate from the actual hip pocket cost, there are far too many other costs to our environmental, health and economic futures.

So what can we do to help reduce the unacceptable costs that have become fundamental to the way we grow, produce and consume food in the world?

Well, thankfully, there is a relatively simple answer! And not only can you reduce your tacit involvement in this failing destructive system, but you will also become healthier, save money and radically improve your personal food security as well.

Let us now look at what I believe could be part of the future of food. We can scale the ideas and concepts promoted in the following chapter to suit a family or community and individualise it to allow for dietary preferences and maximum nutrition and yield. All it takes to achieve these things is some time and effort and an appreciation for what it truly means to act responsibly.

Author's note: All of the above figures from both the FAO and the World Bank are approximations, estimates and assumptions only. Specific data of this nature is challenging to quantify and then apply in global terms. Many figures are selected within what is believed to be the range of possibility and only from specific countries or groups. They may reflect lower or higher actual figures. The costs included are also in no way complete. Many further costs should be included, but specific cost-related data is still yet unknown or unavailable.

I look forward to any insights that will assist us all in providing a far more accurate account of the costs as they stand and implore governments and research bodies to produce their own information and data. I also would appeal to everyone to do their own research and exploration into the true costs of our current food system.

Knowledge is power.

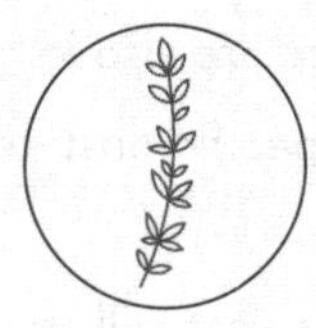

THE FUTURE IS TECHNOGRARIAN

Technology: methods, systems, and devices which are the result of scientific knowledge being used for practical purposes.

– Collins English Dictionary

Any advancement in our understanding of something, or how to do something, has led to technological advancement. The first of these for humanity was learning to control fire and the creation of basic hunting tools. Though primitive compared to today's advancements, they provoked a quantum shift in how human beings fed themselves. That, in turn, radically impacted our biological development for the next two million years.

Since then, we have seen many technological advancements in the way we provide nourishment and sustenance to ourselves and our families. From about 11,000 years ago, we started growing crops and raising animals as we moved away from the far more dangerous pursuit of hunting and gathering. This change provided the foundational stability on which we built empires and civilisations. Other profound technological food production innovations that can be traced back through antiquity are:

1. The use of irrigation to water crops is believed to be almost 6000 years old.
2. The first plough is considered to have been developed more than 3000 years ago.

These game-changing technological advances have had a profound impact on humanity and society's evolution. Without agriculture, humans would not have had the free time to begin to study the world. This, in turn, allowed humans to create even more technology as their understanding and needs grew. This slow agricultural revolution happened over several thousand years, and civilisations rose and fell around it.

In the late 1800s, our agricultural pursuits and the ability to grow our food had what could be considered its most significant impact on humanity. First, life expectancies of those in more developed nations began to increase, followed by similar increases in less developed nations. This then precipitated the most extraordinary explosion in the world population ever recorded. The production demands that this exponential growth placed on our agricultural system were immediate and immense. The pressure to fulfil the demand for greater and greater volumes of food for our rapidly expanding global population underpinned the rise of capitalism and industrialism.

Science and technology drove innovation, and large-scale agriculture was born. Farmers no longer sowed a few acres but hundreds of acres and then thousands of acres. Grains measured in tons became thousands of tons and now millions of tons. If you only take a moment to think back to how we fed ourselves 150 years ago compared to today, the difference is truly breathtaking.

The key issue with many of these incredible developments in agriculture over the last 150 years is that they simply cannot be allowed to continue. The Earth cannot support feeding our ever-growing population in the ways we have developed. Science and technology now need to take us in a new direction. We must take the best of what we have developed and learned from the last 150 years, incorporate that with today's latest advancements and create a new way: one that will not ultimately destroy our planet and leave millions of people around the world sick with chronic disease or without enough food to eat.

We must decentralise these processes, and it needs to become micro-localised. We must acknowledge our personal responsibility for the food we eat, our health and the damage we do to the Earth. Science and technology can now show us how to do this, and many of the things we need to make it a reality are readily available today. While innovations like soil science, plant science, automation, robots and artificial insemination (AI) may still sound like science fiction, the information and technology are available now. It can now be utilised to create the food future we need and deserve.

Science and technology are ready to take us on a new journey on how we grow our food.

Growing our food has been at the centre of human endeavour for the 350 or so generations that have preceded us. Growing our own simple crops fundamentally changed human priorities.

Agrarian: relating to the part of a society that is concerned with cultivating soil and growing crops for food.

It moved us from harvesters of the Earth's bounty to co-creators of it. It stopped our need to be nomadic and the necessity to keep moving from place to place after we had exhausted the resources of our current location. We could set down roots, build homes and raise our families in far safer environments. It allowed us to share and barter with one another and, as such, created trade. It built communities and economies.

Even though this agrarian past drove human evolution along the path we have taken, it also offered us something much richer, deeper and more profound. We were connected to the Earth and the natural world in its purest form. The cycle of birth, growth, decay and death replicated in spring, summer, autumn and winter was innate to who we were and what we did. The health of our land directly impacted our own health and wealth. Our work and effort were seen and felt. It could be smelt and tasted. It could be shared and traded. We had a pure purpose, and we would celebrate those cycles that connected us to them with our families and communities.

We understood a simpler reality. Our fundamental responsibilities were for ourselves and those we loved. We strived for enough, not excess. We were limited to our daylight hours for work, and our work was hard but meaningful. No one ever wondered why they were tending the land and growing crops; their stomachs were their constant reminder.

Agrarianism is at the very core of who we are. Anyone who has ever successfully grown and then enjoyed eating their own produce will attest that the joy derived from the process is unique and profound. It tastes better, it smells better and it feels healthier for you. Those feelings are biologically wired into our subconscious. It is something that we 'know' inside us. Agrarianism has the best tenets of socialism: not as a political ideology but as a philosophy.

As the negative social and economic realities of capitalism become more and more pronounced, humanity must provide a pathway for greater social equality. Concepts like equality of outcome are baked into an agrarian way of life. The best parts of capitalism in the form of barter and trade also come to the fore.

It is not a problematic premise for us to get our heads around, particularly when we consider we have been doing so for thousands of years. Agrarianism in the future will not mean toughing it out in open fields, undertaking back-breaking work. It will mean the creation of abundant, nutritious foods in protected, controlled environments. We can reach back into our past in a way that can carry us into a better, healthier future.

Many people love the idea of a home garden. They understand the many benefits it offers, such as a constant source of tasty and nutritious food. What many people do not know or understand is the quiet revolution that has taken place behind modern homegrown food production scenes. Most people would approach building a home garden in much the same way my grandfather did 80 years ago. Lots of hard physical work, time-intensive and knowledge-hungry. The failure rate of home gardens is exceedingly high. You probably know of someone who has a fenced-off section of a backyard that is either barren or overgrown with weeds and referred to as the 'old veggie garden'.

Technograrian[5]: someone who uses science and technology to grow sustainable, highly nutritious plant-based foods for themselves and their families.

Growing food for ourselves and our family has been quite

the obsession for well over a decade. It started back in 2003 after a shopping trip to our local organic food store. We had just welcomed our third child into the world. With the growing costs of child-raising and a mortgage, we started to notice just how much our weekly organic food shopping was costing us.

To help lessen these costs, we decided we would start a very modest veggie garden at the side of our house. It would measure just a few metres long and about a metre wide. Still, it triggered an explosion of weekend activity. Multiple trips to the local hardware store and garden centre. Many discussions with and advice from store people, and even more grunty, heavy mulch bag lifting, wheelbarrow pushing, shovelling and raking. By Sunday, we wearily but proudly leant on our garden tools and admired the neatly finished wood-trimmed garden bed with its fill of chocolate-brown soil. All the seeds we had planted were now safely tucked away in their earthen homes, having been slightly watered in (we read that was important!). Now we waited for the inevitable bursting forth of eggplants, basil, spinach and broccoli.

Every night we would come home from work and check developments. The first few weeks were slow. As in nothing, really. Not even a tiny green shoot. The next few weeks followed the same disappointing theme. By week nine, we started to wonder if we had forgotten to plant the seeds somehow. But we reassured ourselves that 'things take time' and continued practising patience, extreme patience.

Eventually, the busy life of young parents took over, and we forgot about the garden. Weeks and weeks of hollow disappointment had formed into self-protective disinterest as nothing in the garden appeared remotely inclined to even merely sprout. Many months later, as I was walking past the 'old veggie garden', now thick with weeds and leaf litter, my eye caught a spindly spring onion, standing all alone but proudly tall amongst the weeds. I called Gemma to show her. We looked down upon this miracle of our self-made self-sufficiency. We were saved. We did not speak, but we both knew what this meant. Somehow, in the abject failure that was our first 'veggie garden', that little spring onion was all we needed. It represented the most vital ingredient for any truly worthwhile human pursuit . . . hope.

Since that day, we have kept trying, sometimes failing but always learning. This passion for growing our food has now permeated every aspect of our lives. It has not only dictated where and how we live but has also provided us with the motivation to start health food businesses and other related holistic wellness ventures.

We now have a 200 square metre protected Smart Garden attached to our home in Tasmania. We walk from our living room into our Smart Garden and the incredible bounty of food it provides. It furnishes us with an almost unlimited amount of nutritious produce and also thermally heats our home. It collects rainwater for our drinking water and provides a warm, safe and dry place for our kids to play and for us to drink coffee and read. Last year, in a bed not much larger than our failed first attempt all those years ago, we produced more than 300 kilos of tomatoes. (That is a big difference from a sole spring onion!) A garden is a place of sustenance not only for our bodies with the food it produces but also for our spirits and minds. The smells and verdant colours that surround us compel us to breathe deeply. And stop. And breathe deeply again.

When Gemma and I first met as kids in 1988, we did not question where our food came from. It was the beginning of the emergence of Australian diets taking on a less traditionally British overtone – think meat and three veg with the occasional European respite, for example spaghetti bolognese. I can remember the first time we tried 'new' produce like eggplants or ordered Thai food from a restaurant. If we look back at the expansion of food options available to Australian consumers over the last 30-plus years, it is pretty astonishing.

I grew up in the 1970s and 80s and my father's job was as a frozen food delivery driver. He worked for a company that would deliver up to 12 months of frozen processed food to your door and pack it in your freezer. A family would then never need to eat fresh food, as it was all there – in frozen form. Peas, beans, mixed vegetables, steak, chips, battered fish, hamburgers and much more. Convenience was becoming king, and most of the health and nutritional benefits were now lost to a system of high-speed mass production.

My grandfather is from the silent generation who were born between 1925 and 1945. They were the ones who gave birth to the Baby Boomers and the last to actively produce food within a family unit. I would hear stories of back in the day when Pop and Nan, as children, would barter food produce with other families. Their home garden was necessary for survival, and space was always set aside for food production on any patch of soil available. He and Nan always had a veggie garden and chickens. You could go there and pick anything you needed, any time of the year.

Pop was a professional fisherman who had spent his life since early childhood fishing the sea on the east coast of Australia with his family. They were the epitome of the traditional, hard-working family, spending every day far out to sea and harvesting the abundance of fish, crabs, prawns and lobsters that were available. In those days, the oceans were still genuinely bountiful.

When my grandparents were children, almost all backyards would have some form of food garden. The Great Depression, followed by the Second World War, had made home gardens essential. Starvation was real. Having no money was real. Supply to shops and stores had been reduced to a trickle as supply chains were diverted to the war effort, and rationing was an unavoidable reality.

In those days, growing a family garden was hard physical work, but they benefited from a knowledge pool built on survival and simpler times. The immigrants and refugees from war-torn Europe had brought with them a wealth of agrarian information. They shared their knowledge of composting, soils, plant types, growing methods, harvesting, preserving and storage.

This sharing of knowledge built communities and social structures. Sharing and community were ingrained in every part of the process. Families became more resilient, stronger and healthier. It is worth noting how many of the stories from that time also involve the garden being a source of emotional refuge against the world's calamity. A place where you could go to escape the pain of lost loved ones and help heal by getting 'your hands in the soil', and simply reconnecting with the earth and life.

In the Generational theory, as purported by Neil Howe and William Strauss in their book *The Fourth Turning*, it is reasoned that history repeats itself in cycles of 80 to 100 years. Within each cycle are four generations, or turnings, that follow the pattern of high (new order takes control), awakening (new order is challenged), unravelling (individualism takes hold), and crisis (established social order disintegrates). It follows the 'boom and bust' cycles of the economy and society as a whole. The last bust (or crisis) period culminated with the Great Depression and the Second World War. It was during this period that my grandfather was born. Howe and Strauss place the current time in which we live as a similar repeat of those turbulent 'crisis' times. Any news report would support the fact that we are in a time of great upheaval and change (a Fourth Turning).

As named by Howe and Strauss in 1991, the Millennial generation will likely repeat my grandfather's generation in the cycle.[6]

I believe a by-product of all this uncertainty and upheaval we will face in the next decade will be the necessity of re-establishing things like a home garden for the myriad benefits it offers. In the last 30–40 years, we have enjoyed food sourced through the global supply chains built by Big Ag, Big Chem and even Bigger Business. While this has helped developed countries access cheaper raw commodities from undeveloped countries, it has also led to worker exploitation, unchecked environmental damage, and reduced actual national food production.

Many food commodities we once produced within Australia were not economically viable to produce when commodity prices were pushed lower due to globalism. Suppose we see production move back to the countries that will consume the raw materials. In that case, the increase in labour cost and production costs will be passed directly on to consumers. It would not be unreasonable to expect to see a significant increase in essential fruit and vegetable prices. Already, land values for the last of the remaining productive farmland are increasing at an astonishing rate. Globally, we are losing almost 4 per cent of our arable farmland per year to things like erosion and contamination. Still, our food production needs to grow dramatically.

Our reliance on an industrialised global food system that harms our health, planet and future is not something that will or can continue. Those who do not start building their own Smart Gardens and creating our collective technograrian futures will face higher prices, falling health levels and growing scarcity of supply. Those who do will enjoy fresh produce, better health, food security and the knowledge they have reduced their personal support for and involvement in the destruction of our Earth for future generations.

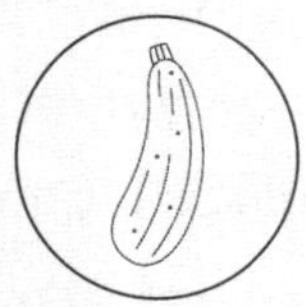

OUR FUTURE FOOD (IN)SECURITY

'The farther we get away from the land, the greater our insecurity.'

– Henry Ford, one of the great industrialists of our time but also a keen observer of human nature

One of the most significant challenges that will face humanity in the following decades will be feeding an ever-growing world population. We already fail to meet this challenge in today's world, with millions of people dying of starvation across the globe every year. According to figures released in 2020, poor nutrition and hunger are responsible for the death of 3.1 million children a year, which is nearly half of all deaths in children under the age of five.[7]

The term '*food security*', by definition, is '*the state of having reliable access to a sufficient quantity of affordable, nutritious food.*'[8] While developed countries take a bountiful produce aisle in the local shopping mall for granted, it is a luxury afforded to very few in global population terms.

While I cannot forecast what could or will be the catalyst for any possible breakdown of our current industrialised food system, the purpose of this chapter is to at least outline some of the more significant potential threats. Hopefully, it will highlight some of the fundamental challenges that our current system faces. Critical issues around public health, environmental damage and economic inequity underscore the system as it stands.

How our food is grown, manufactured and distributed means that there are numerous breakpoints acutely vulnerable to systemic risk. Those risks can be in the form of farming practices that are no longer viable due to the level of environmental damage they cause. That damage has now become so great that they threaten to impact global biosystems to the point of collapse. One example of this is the level of nitrogen and phosphate runoff from large-scale agriculture.

Nitrogen and phosphorus runoff from farming practices enters creeks, rivers and streams and promotes accelerated algae growth. Natural biosystems cannot deal with these increased levels. Huge rises in algae growth hurt not only water quality but food assets and our natural surroundings. It also reduces the oxygen levels that fish and other oceanic life need to survive. Enormous developments of algal growth are called 'algal blooms', and they can seriously lessen or even totally remove all oxygen from water. This promotes diseases in fish and the demise of vast quantities of marine life. Some algal blooms are also unsafe to people since they produce poisons and harmful bacteria. These can make us sick and cause death if we contact or drink the contaminated water or consume spoiled fish or shellfish.

Another area of current commercial food production that carries an inherent risk of collapse is our food supply chains. During the

COVID-19 pandemic, many consumers faced empty supermarket shelves for items such as canned food, pasta and rice. These supply chains rely on chemicals and fossil fuels for production, a human workforce and political stability. While supermarket chains have adopted a 'Just In Time'[9] supply model, this model is grossly underprepared for an event such as the COVID-19 pandemic. With concerned consumers stockpiling food, it only took a matter of days before essential household grocery items became unavailable. Community lockdowns increased fear and generated demand. To combat this, purchase limits were placed on all essential items. In our family's case, these limits were less than our larger than average family requirement. We had to supplement the available limits with produce from our home garden.

Events such as a pandemic, civil and political unrest, or even an unforeseen environmental event could all dramatically impact and even collapse our food supply chains as they stand today. The COVID-19 pandemic has been a wake-up call to the world. These events can and do happen, and many people have been justifiably shaken out of their convenient complacency.

In the definition of 'food security', the term 'nutritious food' is perhaps the most contentious. We assume and are led to believe that what we are purchasing from the fresh produce section of our local supermarket is nutritious. As current research shows, this is, at best, misleading if not dishonest.

It is also worth noting that modern large-scale farming practices are almost myopically focused on only three soil elements required to grow healthy produce, those being nitrogen, phosphorus and potassium. These three elements are vital for productivity, but many other trace elements and minerals are needed to support natural human health. These trace elements and minerals are not replaced in the already depleted soils, which are required to produce season after season of high-density commercial crops. Without the bioavailability of these elements and minerals to the fruits and vegetables grown in this deficient soil, the resulting produce, which may look healthy and robust, lacks the basic building blocks needed for human health.

Food security is currently viewed through the lens of global requirements and sufficiency. The reality is that as the systems we rely upon come under more and more stress, we will be forced to take a far greater active role in creating our own personal food security. On an individual level, we tender the problem of our own personal food security to someone else. We willingly outsource and have very little control over perhaps the most essential requirement for a happy, healthy life – nutritious food.

Without access to sufficient nutritious food, our world becomes much darker and more dangerous. We are lucky to enjoy a current situation where a quick trip to the grocery store can meet our children's food needs. But what happens if any aspect of that changes and that option is not available to you? Will you have made the necessary steps to take control of your own food security and enjoy the peace of mind and untold health benefits that it offers?

The basis of this book is built around a simple concept. It is a reality that cannot be disputed and which we have the benefit of knowing to be true. It is merely this: the closer you are to your food source, the safer, happier and healthier you will be.

WE ARE WHAT WE EAT

'Tell me what you eat, and I will tell you what you are.'

–Jean Anthelme Brillat-Savarin, lawyer, politician, epicure and gastronome

The term 'you are what you eat' first appeared in a 19th-century French cookbook by Jean Anthelme Brillat-Savarin titled *The Physiology of Taste.*[10] As a lawyer, politician, prodigious writer, noted gastronome and lover of food, Brillat-Savarin penned this classic book, which has been in continuous print since 1825. It contained the revelatory phrase, 'Tell me what you eat, and I will tell you what you are.' *The Physiology of Taste* is a landmark work by any measure. It contains incredible recipes, dietary advice (it also promoted avoidance of a high-carb diet!) and even food-related economics. It also looked deeply into the connection between our food and culture and, more specifically, how the food we consume speaks to the people we are.

In 1863, German philosopher Ludwig Feuerbach wrote 'man is what he eats' in his book *Concerning Spiritualism and Materialism.*[11] As a promoter of Anthroposophical Materialism and a social democrat, he believed that social change and revolution did not happen because of human understanding or intelligence, but by producing things that matter the most to us and exchanging them.

As a philosopher, Feuerbach believed that actual societal change is only ever driven through changes in the production of goods and their exchange. He felt that meaningful real change in society is not prefaced by endless circular discussion and critiques on how we change or what we need to change. If we look back throughout history, we can see that technological developments, driven by societal needs, have brought about profound changes in our societies and economies.

In the early 1900s, the phrase 'you are what you eat' is believed to have appeared as part of a beef advertisement in the *Bridgeport Telegraph*. In 1940, nutritionist Victor Lindlahr published his book titled, *You Are What You Eat: How to win and keep health with diet*,[12] which brought the phrase to mass public consciousness. Lindlahr was a strong advocate for the premise that food controlled health and believed that 'cheap foodstuffs cause ninety per cent of the diseases known to man'. *You Are What You Eat* also actively promoted the concept that 'food is medicine'.

I felt the need to offer some historical outline of the phrase's emergence and its more significant conceptual ramifications. If we see the term as accurate and 'we are what we eat', how should we evaluate ourselves today against that presumption?

We live in a day and age where convenience is king, due primarily to our ostensibly busy and highly stressed lifestyles. The need to time-compress even the most fundamental aspects of our human necessities, like feeding ourselves, has been a critical driver in designing and creating most of the items we find in our grocery store. Many of us innately appreciate, and can even romanticise, the smells and tastes of freshly baked bread but cannot find the time in our busy schedules to even consider making bread for ourselves. In Australia, we have had grocery suppliers importing premade bread and muffin products from as far away as Ireland.

The same large grocery suppliers ultimately came under the scrutiny of governmental oversight as concerned shoppers questioned the labelling of the bread as being 'freshly baked'[13]. Apparently, there was a part of the final process of baking that was completed in Australia, so the company deemed the use of 'freshly baked' to be appropriate. While technically, this statement was right, it shows the level to which our food system's corporate powers will knowingly mislead and misrepresent. Had those same bread and muffin products carried information about the fact that they had been made several months earlier, in a country halfway around the world, consumers may have made different purchase decisions.

Economically, these products could be sold at significantly lower prices than Australian-made products, impacting local bread manufacturing. Australian manufacturing has declined for decades due to high wages and operational costs and the incredibly high costs of compliance required to manufacture 'safe' food products. Though necessary to meet minimum safety standards for importation, products made in other countries are often not subject to the same checks and balances that Australian ones are required by law to adhere to.[14] This creates an enormous cost burden for local manufacturers and, in many cases, a situation in which they cannot compete. This then economically impacts manufacturing jobs and opportunities for people within our country.

Let's look at the potential carbon mile impact of the journey from Ireland to Australia. It is easy to see how those bread and muffin products would have unnecessarily generated carbon dioxide into the atmosphere when considering the carbon emissions generated by transportation alone. Assuming these products were shipped to Australia, it is worth noting that international shipping generates 3.1 per cent of all greenhouse gas emissions.[15] This unnecessary journey would add to the environmental and societal damages of climate change. A journey of more than 15,000 kilometres for a product that would sell for less than $5 seems crazy by any measure. Still, millions of cheap products are transported huge distances around the world every single day. The environmental impact of food carbon miles is only now being calculated and factored into the higher actual cost of the products we purchase. Suppose we assume these products were packaged in single-use plastic bags and made from genetically modified wheat grown with high pesticide and herbicide levels. In that case, we begin to see our current food system's real cost to the environment.

We also need to consider that those bread and muffin products potentially travelled for many weeks to get to Australia and are subject to some anti-spoilage regime. Perhaps that involved weeks or months of refrigeration, or the addition of several chemicals to increase shelf life? It is difficult to comprehend just how 'freshly baked' bread and muffin products survive for that extended period, let alone are presented to shoppers with all the attributes of freshly baked bread.

Long-life food production uses a vast array of means and chemicals to promote extended shelf life. In many cases, the actual health and environmental impacts of the processes and chemicals are unknown. Many chemicals used in bread production are banned in some countries and regions yet not in others. *The Guardian* newspaper featured a story in May 2019 titled, 'Banned Bread: Why does the US allow additives that Europe says are unsafe?'. In the story, writer Troy Farah looked at many chemical additives linked to health problems and cancer:

> Some of these chemicals, used as optional whiteners, dough conditioners and rising agents, may be harmful to human health. Potassium bromate, a potent oxidiser that helps bread rise, has been linked to kidney and thyroid cancers in rodents. Azodicarbonamide (ACA), a chemical that forms bubbles in foams and plastics like vinyl, is used to bleach and leaven dough – but when baked, it, too, has been linked to cancer in lab animals.

However, it's not just the so-called dough conditioners that need questioning, Farah reported:

> Two preservatives, BHA and BHT, subject to strong EU restrictions, are widely used in baked goods in the US. These emulsifiers keep fats and oils from spoiling. Still, the International Agency for Research on Cancer suggests there is sufficient evidence that BHA causes tumour growth in lab animals, with more limited evidence for the same in BHT.[16]

Troy Farah also noted that funding for research into the additives used in our food products like bread is tough for laboratories to generate. Many government bodies are reluctant to place bans without this indisputable evidence. Unfortunately, it usually takes a public health outcry or civil litigation to force them to implement these bans.

We have just used one single bread and muffin product made in Ireland and sold in Australia as an example of our globalised food system's real economic, health and environmental consequences. Around the globe, this example is mirrored in thousands, if not millions, of products we purchase every year.

If indeed 'we are what we eat', then we face a grim current and future reality as our simple bread example shows. Let's look at those real economic, health, social and environmental costs in greater detail.

THE END OF GLOBALISM

Any research into the origins of the produce we find in our local shopping aisle will often show that it has come from countries and regions on the other side of the world. Those places of origin may or may not have had any oversight of how the food was produced in terms of pesticide and herbicide use, hygiene, nutritional values and environmental impact. Already the majority of the world's population rely on some level of imported food.[17] In 2019 there were an estimated 135 million people in 55 countries facing acute levels of hunger. In 2018 it was 118 million people in 53 countries.[18] Due to various reasons, be they economic, internal conflicts or political unrest, these nations must import food for their populations' basic sustenance.

The United States already imports more than $110 billion worth of food annually,[19] despite its agricultural sector being one of the largest in the world. These imports are, in most cases, an opportunity to offer consumers greater choice and diversification of produce. Demand for new and novel products from developed nations has poorer nations exporting their products for higher developed nations' prices. This denies the products' availability to their local markets as they cannot afford the same prices.

With the advent of global supply chains and globalised food production, fresh produce may undertake a journey across the globe after harvest. This product's journey can take many days, if not weeks, to finally arrive in the country in which it is to be consumed. Just the required energy use in this type of globalised supply chain is astonishing, from oil-based fossil fuels for ships, trucks and farm equipment, to the cost of long-term cold storage and warehousing. The fact the system works to supply us with the produce, with such an incredible array of moving parts and from all corners of the globe, is a credit to human ingenuity.

The model corporations use for the supply chain for food and consumables is referred to in management terms as the 'Just In Time' (JIT) model.[20] It is where supply chains operate to get the end product to the consumer just in time, before spoilage. Anyone who has ever purchased fresh produce at a grocery store would have experienced the reality of this firsthand. Have you ever bought a ripe, healthy-looking item and brought it home to see it degrade and spoil over the next 24 to 48 hours to a point where it is completely inedible?

This is the 'Just In Time' supply chain management in action. Some people will take the spoiled product back and demand a refund, but the vast majority will not. The grocery chains know that. The methods used to keep a vegetable or fruit in that condition for such a protracted period will involve everything from extended cold storage to gas-based chemical ripening processes.

The JIT model has economic benefits to the corporate bottom line by reducing their costs. Still, it also has an inherent risk because the JIT model has minimal capacity and elasticity to handle shocks and events outside the business-as-usual circumstances. During the COVID-19 pandemic, the model showed how it could fail as supermarkets were overwhelmed with panic buying and shelves became empty overnight.

Research firm McKinsey issued an update on the potential problems with the JIT model. They speculated that, due to global uncertainty around many vital issues, perhaps the JIT model needed to make way for a new supply chain model: a model designed more specifically for the current world we find ourselves living in. This new model for supply chain management would be more accurately described as the 'Just In Case' model.[21]

PANDEMIC IMPACT

Many of us in the developed world did not feel the dramatic effects of the 2007–08 food shortage. Still, its impact on the developing world was considerable. The World Bank reported that in the three years leading up to 2008, global food prices rose a staggering 83 per cent:

> The food crisis appeared to explode overnight, reinforcing fears that there are just too many people in the world. But according to the FAO, with record grain harvests in 2007, there is more than enough food in the world to feed everyone – at least 1.5 times the current demand. In fact, over the last 20 years, food production has risen steadily at over 2.0% a year, while the rate of population growth has dropped to 1.14% a year. The population is not outstripping the food supply. 'We're seeing more people hungry and at greater numbers than before,' says World Hunger Program's executive director Josette Sheeran. There is food on the shelves, but people are priced out of the market.[22]

The food supply crisis of 2008 showed that the global food production system, while appearing to function efficiently, is still susceptible to systemic system shocks that can quickly cause a rapid rise in food prices. This crisis would act as a forerunner to what would be the biggest unexpected shock to our global food supply chain that we have experienced in our lifetime – the COVID-19 pandemic.

The COVID-19 pandemic caused almost all countries worldwide to lock down to control the spread of the virus. The impacts on farmers, agricultural supplies, factories, transportation and supermarkets, and the many other moving parts in the complex web that is our global food supply chain, have been pervasive and frightening. The pandemic's impact on the shipping industry and international transportation has been profound. Many ports were closed to try to stop the further importation of the virus from infected ship crew members. There have been outbreaks worldwide that can be traced back to ship crews. The living conditions aboard these large vessels acted as the perfect petri dish for virus infection rates.[23]

These restrictions to necessary trade between and within countries severely restricted and, in some cases, stopped existing supply chains. This can be seen in the empty shelves at supermarkets for storable food items like rice, pasta and canned goods. The panic of the pandemic caused radical fluctuations in the buying patterns of consumers. Pre-lockdown concerns saw consumers panic buying and hoarding essential items. This created a demand spike that the system could not cope with, led to empty shelves, and limited the number of things consumers could purchase. During these lockdowns, consumer numbers fell and stores remained empty as the general population, now confined to their home, radically reduced their in-store shopping habits and consumption.

At the time of writing this book, we still see the net effect this 'closing of economies' has had on aspects of our society like our food supply. With anything of this nature, the impact will initially be felt most by marginal communities. People without sufficient food supplies or the financial means to stock up will be at the most significant risk. The pandemic will have a short-term deflationary impact on things like fresh produce as products in the system will be fast approaching use-by dates. Retailers will need to lower prices to assist the sale of these items during lockdowns.

Ultimately, though, I see it having a primarily inflationary impact with rapidly rising prices as we manage the disruption to production that will create colossal inventory and capacity shortages. Of the limited supplies of basic commodities that become available, more affluent countries will have the purchasing power to capture large parts of these supplies. This leaves poorer countries to fend for themselves with the commodities produced within the borders of their own country. These higher prices on the limited products available will have to be passed on to consumers. With the economic impact of the virus leading to massive global job losses, even essential items will become too expensive for many populations.

Those of us who have actively worked towards and taken responsibility for creating some insurance around our own personal food supply will be well rewarded in the coming months and years through initiatives like a Smart Garden.

NATURAL DISASTERS

In a report by the FAO in 2015, titled 'The Impact of Natural Hazards and Disasters on Agriculture and Food Security and Nutrition',[24] it was highlighted that very little information had been recorded about the real impact that events like droughts, floods, storms such as hurricanes and cyclones, earthquakes, tsunamis and volcanic eruptions have on global agriculture. The report researched 78 of these events from 2003 to 2013 and found some very frightening insights.

It showed that while these events have a devastating impact on the populations and location or regions in which they occurred, the devastation to the agricultural sector within the geographical area amounted to 22 per cent of the economic damage. This was further broken down into the two key areas that suffer the most significant impact: crop destruction and livestock deaths. According to the FAO:

> The findings show that the 78 disasters caused a total of US$140 billion in damage and losses on all sectors, of which US$30 billion was on the agriculture sector and subsectors. On average, agriculture absorbs 22 per cent of the total economic impact caused by natural hazards.[25]

Perhaps the most sobering information within the report shows that crop destruction amounted to 89 per cent of the economic losses.

Crop destruction was also shown to cause a dramatic and immediate impact on the accessibility of food within the region. While the need for imported products to fulfil those food requirements rose exponentially, the region's earned income, post–natural disaster event, fell exponentially.

It is the very nature of some natural disaster events to strike without warning, and their devastation can be total. Alternatively, events like droughts can affect significant global areas over many years. In some cases, the viability of any future agricultural production simply ceases as the infrastructure and human capital needed to create products leave the area and relocate to places of more opportunity.

Data shows that the impact of natural disasters can affect productivity for decades after the event.[26]

Let's look at the data of the occurrence of natural disaster–defined events over previous decades. It is generally considered to show a rise in the number of meteorologically determined events like drought and floods. There is no data to support that the incidence of earthquakes and volcanic activity is increasing. What is rising is the economic damage caused by these events when we factor in population, urbanisation and agricultural impact. The cost of these events increases as more and more people are directly and indirectly affected by them. Government response programs are costing more and more as the number and scale of these events increase, often allowing little respite between events.

The data shows that the number of these meteorological events is increasing in our temperate climate zones. The incidence of natural disasters in temperate climate zones will have the most significant impact on our global food production.[27] The agricultural land within these zones offers the best soil and climate conditions

Significant global natural catastrophe events 2019

Monetary figures are in US dollars.

for large-scale cropping and agriculture. Soil nutrients are generally higher and rainfall patterns are consistent. Temperate climate zones also have distinct seasons. This helps mitigate pestilence, with winter temperatures serving to control insect outbreaks and crop-destroying bacteria and moulds.[28]

If the climate change models used by scientific and government agencies worldwide hold true, the frequency of weather-related natural disasters will increase. Their future impact on our food supply systems will be substantial. It is not hard to imagine how increased rainfall volume causes catastrophic flooding to crucial agricultural areas. Those areas will suffer total crop losses from the event and the destruction of critical infrastructure, and, more importantly, the loss and erosion of vital topsoil and nutrients. This would further reduce our already dramatically decreasing agricultural land and further exacerbate the difficulties the agricultural sector is facing to supply produce to consumers.

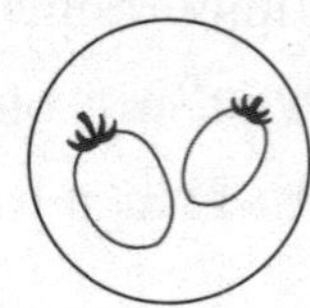

FOOD LOSS AND WASTAGE

'Feel what it's like to truly starve, and I guarantee that you'll forever think twice before wasting food.'

– Criss Jami, existentialist philosopher, essayist and songwriter

The global economic cost of food wastage, and the negative impact of what it costs to produce and then dispose of wasted food, is estimated by the FAO to be just over US$1 trillion dollars annually. The actual economic impact of food wastage is much higher. When we consider the natural capital cost, as in the cost of the environmental damage – through the pollution to the atmosphere, water and land, and the damage inflicted on biodiversity and ecological systems – we need to add another US$2.1 trillion of loss. This food wastage also generates social costs as it negatively impacts the health and livelihoods of populations around the world.

Suppose we also include those social costs from the sheer volume of global food wastage. That would add a further

US$2.33 trillion. So best estimates place the total economic, environmental and social cost of food wastage at roughly US$4.8 trillion. Currently, the global food system's monetary value is estimated to have an economic benefit of US$4–8 trillion. That would then illuminate the issue we have: any financial benefits are undermined by trillions of dollars of cost of what we waste producing the initial economic benefit. That is simply a completely unsustainable system.

These numbers come from reports on food wastage that the FAO has delivered to the United Nations. When compiling a list of costs around factors like natural capital costs, they use a full-cost accounting method that relies on assumptions and estimates. The volume and scale of data involved in calculating the actual cost of devastating environmental damage are immense. The FAO does speak to this and believes the figures they have come up with most likely would represent an underestimate. Logically, how do you value thousands of acres of Amazonian rainforest that now no longer exist? Or, in the case of the social costs, what price do you place on the life of a child who has died of starvation when millions of tons of food have been ploughed into landfill?

To highlight the staggering reality these numbers point to, we must look at these costs concerning how we currently purchase our food and the devastation to which we become complicit. The FAO reports:

> Food loss and waste have significant negative food-security, economic and environmental impacts. The value of annual food loss and waste at the global level is estimated at USD 1 trillion. Food loss and waste may decrease food availability in the market, which may increase food prices and reduce low-income consumers' capacity to access food.

> Moreover, suppose the food quality deteriorates so severely that the food must be sold at a lower price or even discarded. In that case, the livelihood of farmers and producers is adversely affected. Food loss and waste represent wastage of the water, land, energy and other natural resources used to produce food.
>
> The resources used to produce food that is eventually lost or wasted account for approximately 4.4 gigatons of greenhouse gas emissions (CO_2 equivalent) annually, making food loss and waste the world's third-largest emitter, after only China and the United States.[29]

It is estimated that the US spends an alarming $218 billion to grow, process, transport and dispose of food that is never eaten.[30] That is more than the nominal GDP of a country like New Zealand (2018). Supply chain inefficiencies and the inability to get products to consumers quickly are significant contributing factors to this startling statistic.

In a world where millions are dying from starvation every year, it highlights the divide between rich and developing nations. In developing nations, food wastage is higher during harvest, processing and transport. A lack of efficient infrastructure and the primary use of manual labour plays a prominent role. In developed nations, food loss and wastage mainly occur around consumption, with food being uneaten or left to spoil.

Data sourced from the Australian government Department of Agriculture, Water and the Environment states that one-third of all the food produced in the world is ultimately wasted. It also found that 25 per cent of the water used in agriculture is wasted irrigating food that will never be eaten. One uneaten or wasted hamburger squanders the equivalent amount of water as a 90-minute shower.[31]

It is estimated that global food production makes up 26 per cent of greenhouse gas emissions,[32] and 18 per cent of those emissions come from the post-harvest supply chains. Interestingly, fuel used in transportation only makes up a small (6 per cent) part of this figure, with wastage and packaging having the greatest impact. If food waste were a country, it would be the third-largest emitter of greenhouse gases, behind the USA and China.[33]

FOOD CONTAMINATION

On 31 July 2001, young Kevin Kowalcyk woke with a mild fever and diarrhoea. The next day, his mother noticed blood traces in his diarrhoea, so she took him to their local hospital's emergency department. Over the following few days, tests confirmed that two-year-old Kevin was suffering from *E. coli* O157:H7, a foodborne illness that affects more than 96,000 Americans on average every year.[34]

Kevin's condition worsened. He soon developed hemolytic uremic syndrome, a condition that destroys platelets and blood vessels, including the small ones in the kidneys, brain, heart and intestines. On 11 August, after days of relentless physical destruction, Kevin died, his body having suffered total tissue death of both his large and small intestine.

The heartbroken family now desperately needed answers on how and why their precious two-year-old had been taken from them. Investigations would conclude that Kevin had contracted the *E. coli* bacteria from a beef hamburger the family had purchased for him at a local restaurant.

Inspiringly, Kevin's mother, Barbra Kowalcyk, went on to form the Center for Foodborne Illness Research and Prevention. She was instrumental in creating the changes made to the US Food and

Drug Administration's (FDA) *Food Safety Modernisation Act* which became law in 2011.

The World Bank reported in 2018 that the economic burden of contaminated food was estimated to cost low- and middle-income countries US$95 billion in lost productivity and US$15 billion in treatment costs.[35] These figures, though, do not show the true human cost of food contamination.

Here are some startling facts from the World Health Organization in 2020:

- Access to sufficient amounts of safe and nutritious food is key to sustaining life and promoting good health.
- Unsafe food containing harmful bacteria, viruses, parasites or chemical substances causes more than 200 diseases – ranging from diarrhoea to cancers.
- An estimated 600 million – almost 1 in 10 people in the world – fall ill after eating contaminated food and 420,000 die every year, resulting in the loss of 33 million healthy life years (DALYs).
- US$110 billion is lost each year in productivity and medical expenses resulting from unsafe food in low- and middle-income countries.
- Children under five years of age carry 40 per cent of the foodborne disease burden, with 125,000 deaths every year.
- Diarrhoeal diseases are the most common illnesses resulting from consuming contaminated food, causing 550 million people to fall ill and 230,000 deaths every year.
- Food safety, nutrition and food security are inextricably linked. Unsafe food creates a vicious cycle of disease and malnutrition, particularly affecting infants, young children, the elderly and the sick.

- Foodborne diseases impede socioeconomic development by straining healthcare systems and harming national economies, tourism and trade.[36]

Let us put just some of the above numbers in perspective. Estimates show that more people die from food contamination in the world than from homicide.[37] Around the world, over half as many people who fall ill with influenza (1 billion) will fall ill from food contamination (550 million).[38]

Food contamination can happen at any point during the food production process. Research shows that while the responsibility must ultimately be with food producers, with the adoption of more stringent hygiene controls, food contamination can often occur close to or at the point of consumption. Serious foodborne disease outbreaks have occurred on every continent in the past decade and have been amplified in some cases by global trade.

In 2017–18, ready-to-eat meat produced in South Africa was contaminated with *Listeria monocytogenes*. The contamination resulted in 1060 cases of listeriosis and 216 deaths. This meat product was shipped to 15 other countries and required an international response to implement risk management procedures.

Contamination can occur to food products from bacteria, viruses, parasites and prions. One of the leading causes of increasing bacterial food contamination is the overuse of antibiotics in livestock production. Data from a recent FDA report highlights the use of antibiotics in US livestock production:

> The data shows that, of the more than 6.1 million kilograms of medically important antibiotics sold to US farmers in 2019, an estimated 41% were intended for use in cattle, 42% in swine, 10% in turkeys, and 3% in chickens.[39]

We have also recently witnessed that food contamination can occur via feedstock that is fed to livestock. Prions are an infectious agent composed of proteins and are linked to neurodegenerative diseases. Bovine spongiform encephalopathy, or mad cow disease, is a prion disease and associated with Creutzfeldt–Jakob disease in humans. It is believed that consuming high-risk material like 'brain tissue' is the most likely way prion agents infect humans.

Interestingly, I found this on the *Medical News Today* website regarding the benefits of eating cow brains:

> Brain meat contains omega-3 fatty acids and nutrients. The latter include phosphatidylcholine and phosphatidylserine, which are good for the nervous system. The antioxidants obtained by eating brain meat are also helpful in protecting the human brain and spinal cord from damage.[40]

Perhaps we need to review what we eat when considering aspects of our food production system like food contamination. The US Department of Agriculture (USDA) has stated that 70 per cent of food poisoning that occurs in the US is from animal flesh products, and the Environmental Protection Agency (EPA) has stated that up to 70 per cent of all food purchased in the US contains toxic chemicals! I really have to wonder when these types of statistics will start to radically change how we grow and consume food. How many more stories like young Kevin's need to fill our newsfeeds before we appreciate the situation's urgency?

We need to take back responsibility and control of at least part of our personal food requirement; it is not only urgent but desperately essential. If your family's health and food quality and security are of even the slightest importance to you, growing your own food is simply the best way to insure yourself against all the risks and dangers we now face.

PLASTIC USAGE

Though plastic was first invented in 1907 when Belgian–American chemist Leo Baekeland created Bakelite, its use has become ubiquitous in our modern society. Many food producers have resorted to excessive packaging and plastic wraps to improve product quality and reduce spoilage and wastage. Plastics from packaging made up 42 per cent of plastic pollution and amounted to a bewildering 146 million tons in 2015.

This type of packaging is extremely harmful to the environment and requires petrochemicals in its manufacture. Numerous media articles and related public concerns have given this issue more focus in recent times. Manufacturers and retailers are confronted with a choice between two evils. The first is the cost of wastage of food products that suffer reduced shelf lives without the use of plastics. The second is the environmental impact of these plastics once they are placed in landfill or, worse, cause environmental pollution by entering natural habitats and waterways.

Suppose we unpack (pun intended) this issue further. In that case, we see that wastage will affect the business's bottom line through lost revenue and the costs associated with disposing of wasted food products. The economic and environmental cost related to the packaging does not impact the operational costs of the business. So companies are quick to position themselves on the side of increased use of plastics and packaging while acknowledging that their use of these is not ideal.

Until we have a situation where the real cost of using these plastics and packaging appears as a cost to businesses, it's hard to imagine we will see the funding to develop things like reduced plastic requirements, faster supply chain systems, and biodegradable packaging alternatives. In Australia over the last five years, we have seen that consumer and environmental groups calling for changes to the amount of single-use plastic bags in stores has had an impact. Supermarkets began to charge a nominal fee for the bags, and consumers can now avoid the cost by reusing bags or purchasing environmentally friendly reusable shopping bags.

In a 2020 report, researcher Emmanuel Bonnard outlined the environmental cost of plastic usage:

> Human beings have produced nearly ten billion tons of plastic since 1950, of which only 12% has been incinerated and 9% recycled. The rest has ended up in the environment. At best, in 'controlled' landfills where waste is often buried and more or less insulated from the ground, at least in developed countries. And at worst, in illegal landfills, where it decomposes in the open air, producing methane, or directly into the environment, where it is dispersed by wind, rain and water.
>
> Current practices in plastic waste elimination are environmentally unsatisfactory. Incineration uses large amounts of (mainly fossil-fuel) energy, and burning plastic produces CO2 and other pollutants. While we now know how to process incineration residues (for example, by using them as sub-layers in road construction), we continue to burn PVC, which emits dioxin. This is far from the norm in emerging and intermediate countries. Incineration goes unsupervised and emits highly toxic pollutants such as dioxin and benzene into the atmosphere, usually close to urban areas.
>
> Neither do landfills offer guarantees of environmental respect. The decomposition of plastic into micro-particles, combined with the release of acid (from non-recycled batteries, for example), emits extremely toxic substances that damage our endocrine systems and are thought to cause cancer.

> In a recent landmark report, the World Wildlife Fund (WWF) estimated that 37% of world plastic waste is not managed ecologically. Rather than being collected, it is discarded in the environment or dumped in uncontrolled landfills. The situation is a source of extreme concern, as 80% of this waste will pollute ecosystems and the oceans in particular. The WWF estimates that 80% of sea pollution comes from terrestrial sources.[41]

Until the environmental damage of the estimated 8.3 billion tons of plastics produced since the 1950s[42] is presented as a financial cost to the producers and users of these plastics, will we see any marked change? Perhaps a plastic tax like the one introduced in Ireland in 2002 is one possible answer. Ireland introduced the tax and has seen a reduction from plastics being 5 per cent of its landfill in 2001 to just 0.13 per cent in 2015.[43]

Almost 50 per cent of plastic use occurs in the way we store and consume food. Millions of single-use plastic water bottles and plastic shopping bags are being used every few minutes worldwide, and the volume is growing. In fact, it is believed that nearly 2 million plastic bags are used every minute around the world![44] The truth is that only approximately 9 per cent of plastics are recycled, and it is not cost-effective to recycle plastic.[45] It makes consumers feel better as they separate plastic waste into their council-facilitated recycling bin, but plastic is currently more than likely sent to a more impoverished Asian nation for stockpiling until a buyer can be found. Even these countries, such as Malaysia, are drowning under the deluge of 'recycled' plastics. They are now banning further container ships from dumping even more Western-derived recycling.

Most plastics are made from crude oil. If global crude oil prices fall, the manufacturing cost for virgin (new) plastic is reduced, making the cost of recycling plastics even more prohibitive. The whole push for community recycling programs is the extraordinarily successful attempt by the plastics industry to place the responsibility of plastic pollution firmly at the feet of consumers. While the corporations whose products create millions and millions of tons of plastic pollution are left to pocket profits, the consumers are placated with 'community clean-up programs' created with corporate spin.

The actuality is that recycling is a myth. It keeps consumers from understanding the actual destruction that every piece of plastic they are using is creating. Plastic left to pollute the environment does not go away; it is worn down to produce smaller and smaller particles known as microplastics. Studies show that these microplastics can now be found in every waterway and landmass around the globe. They are not only devastating marine life, but they are also currently in the farmland soils that grow our food and in the air we breathe. Both large and small plastics will take hundreds if not thousands of years to break down sufficiently to no longer be a threat.

According to new research from the University of Victoria in Canada, the average American adult consumes 126–142 tiny particles of plastic every day, and inhales another 132–170 plastic bits daily too.[46]

When the total economic, environmental and social cost of plastic use is considered, there can be no argument that it represents an issue that requires urgent and immediate attention. Governments are beginning to act, with more than 1000 different plastic-use mitigation policies adopted by governments and local councils worldwide in 2019. Unfortunately, at the rate at which we are producing plastic and the speed at which it finds its way into our environments, we have already run out of time. Oceana.org estimates that the equivalent of one council garbage truck's worth of plastics is dumped into the oceans alone every single minute![47]

We can no longer be complicit in environmental destruction at this level. We must begin to see that one way we can radically reduce our personal plastic use is to become far more self-sufficient in producing and supplying our own food. Just the act of producing 20–30 per cent of the food we require in our own home gardens would reduce our plastic usage by potentially more than 100 kilograms every year. Let's consider all the benefits that personal responsibility for our food supply and production grants us. It becomes difficult to deny that it is not only a great idea but a moral imperative.

CREATING COMPASSION FROM WASTE

In 2018, Alessandro Demaio from EAT, a Norway-based NGO focused on tackling world hunger, gave the following response about the challenges that our current food system creates for the world:

> Food is, in one way or another, linked to all UN's 17 Sustainable Development Goals. As a doctor, it deeply concerns me that more than 800 million people go hungry, and more than two billion are overweight or obese worldwide. These numbers are accompanied by a ballooning epidemic of diet-related and preventable diseases such as diabetes, heart disease and cancers. Food is our number one global health challenge and a formidable climate threat. We're not only producing what makes us sick and destroys the planet, but we also continue to subsidize it with billions of dollars annually. It is the world's poor and the communities who are least responsible for creating them who are disproportionately affected by these trends.[48]

We are faced with many complex issues regarding food loss and wastage and how that could alleviate the problems of hunger in the world. The first issue is around the actual definition of food loss and wastage. The definition is not consistent between government agencies and NGOs, so the development of any unified policy action becomes more difficult from the outset.

We need to create far more equity in distributing our food supply. The repurposing of food loss and waste offers an enormous opportunity. Key areas that can help rebalance food supply equity are meal sizes, supply chain inefficiencies and feedstocks. Meal sizes in developed countries, particularly in food service, have grown over the last two decades. As restaurants want to increase perceived value, plate sizes and meal volume have increased. This has led to a global rise in diet-related health issues. These increases are often by way of nutritionally void carbohydrates. Still, it has also resulted in high amounts of food wastage with the food returned to kitchens uneaten. This wastage can be repurposed into feedstock and soil-regenerating composts.

An animal feedstock is made up of the parts of crops that are fit for human consumption. Currently, more than half of the annual crop calories in the US are used for stock feed. On a global scale, 36 per cent of the calories produced by the world's crops are being used for animal feed, and only 12 per cent of those feed calories ultimately contribute to the human diet (as meat and other animal products).[49]

Food wastage can be recycled for products like animal feedstocks and green manure. South Korea, Japan and Taiwan lead the way with innovative and highly effective 'food waste to animal feed' strategies. In South Korea, it is illegal to dump food waste into landfill. In 2013 the government introduced a program to supply all Korean families with a biodegradable bag used to collect food waste and scraps and turn it into compost and animal feed. This initiative now sees South Korea recycling and repurposing 95 per cent of its food waste.[50]

During my research into the issues and facts around food loss and waste, I began to better appreciate the difficulty in attaining reliable figures due to the complexity of the problem and its sheer scale. Suppose we work from the mean of the data presented. In that case, we can assume that somewhere in the vicinity of one-third of our food production, or more specifically, calorie production, is wasted globally. The two main areas where waste occurs are at a consumer level (e.g. uneaten or spoiled produce) and losses that arise due to production processes.

It is inspiring to see food waste programs like the one in South Korea and the plastic bag tax in Ireland. It shows that there is sufficient will in the general community to adopt policies of change and commit to their success.

OUR FALLING LEVELS OF NUTRITION

'We think of an orange as a constant, but the reality is it isn't. You would have to eat eight oranges today to get the same amount of vitamin A your grandparents got from a single orange. And you would need to eat five to get the same level of iron.'

– Tim Lang, Emeritus Professor of Food Policy, Centre For Food Policy, City University London

Under the green-hued LED lights and automatic misting systems of your local grocery store's fruit and vegetable aisle lies a growing problem. As we become more aware of the real impacts that food and nutrition have on our health and wellbeing, many people are trying to eat more 'clean'. We're seeing a shift towards more fresh fruit and vegetables as a percentage of the average weekly grocery shop. Still, the reality is that the benefits of this change are much less than we think.

A University of California study showed that vegetables can lose

15 to 55 per cent of their vitamin C in just a week after being picked. Some spinach can lose 90 per cent within the first 24 hours. Most fresh produce can lose approximately 30 per cent of its nutritional value in just three days after harvest.[51]

In a research study into the impact of transportation, storage and retail shelf conditions on lettuce quality and phytonutrient losses in the supply chain, the South African government found a typical Crisp Head or Iceberg lettuce showed the following losses of trace minerals at the average point of purchase: iron reduced by 48.8 per cent, zinc 34 per cent, manganese 49.7 per cent, copper 79.8 per cent and boron 23 per cent.[52]

Many factors come into play during harvesting, transport, storage and retail shelf display that can further exacerbate these losses, such as temperature fluctuations and handling methods. Rough handling and machine processing can easily damage the natural protective skin of fresh produce. Those abrasions, cuts and damage are a point of oxidation and vital moisture loss and increase susceptibility to bacterial infection. Temperature variations from ambient harvest temperatures to cold storage to air-conditioned retail displays are also a point at which produce can suffer the impact of cellular breakdown and the loss of nutrients.[53]

Research suggests that some macronutrients and minerals do have more stability to withstand the processes of modern supply chains.[54] It is the micronutrients that are much more susceptible to significant losses.

While fresh produce is infinitely better for us than processed foods, no matter the source, the perception is that our fresh produce is far healthier for us than it is. Study after study has marked the decline in critical essential vitamins and minerals across almost all fresh food categories. This is due to a range of issues primarily centred around soil health, chemical usage and the time it takes to get produce into stores. While annual sales of certified organic produce grow, there is still no mechanism to measure the soil quality and 'harvest to the consumer' timeline of this produce.

Organically grown produce cultivated in nutrient-depleted soil, transported in cold storage and shipped halfway around the world will still only contain a small portion of its original or potential nutrient density. While the premium you will pay for organically certified produce is justifiable for many reasons, and not least of which is its more sustainable production methods, it is still a far cry from the benefits you would receive by producing the same vegetable or fruit using the Smart Garden method we will discuss later.

With current food production methods, we need to be consuming at least three or four times the volume of fresh produce to attain the same level of nutrients, minerals and vitamins available to people just two generations ago.[55]

A landmark study published in 2004 in the *Journal of the American College of Nutrition* analysed US Department of Agriculture nutritional data from both 1950 and 1999 for 43 different vegetables and fruits. It found 'reliable declines' in the amount of protein, calcium, phosphorus, iron, riboflavin (vitamin B2) and vitamin C over the past 50 years. This declining nutritional content was attributed to the prevalence of agricultural practices designed to improve traits (size, growth rate, pest resistance) other than nutrition.[56]

With an exponential rise in the diseases of affluence, such as heart disease and diabetes, it has become apparent that the lack of access to quality nutrients and vitamins via our diets is not an issue of cost per se. Wealthy economies have enjoyed falling prices in many cases for fresh food items. Still, these downward price pressures are often the result of the buying power of large grocery buyers and distributors.

In general, any improved agricultural production efficiencies are immediately negated by reductions in the price paid to farmers. These efficiencies also come from the increased use of farming practices that are not sustainable, such as increased chemical usage. This current cycle of downward price pressure driving reduced produce quality, and the adoption of unsustainable farm practices, will, ironically, ultimately lead to much higher consumer prices.

I anticipate we will see an exponential increase in the price of fresh food items in the medium-term. Farmers will soon experience a raft of newly implemented climate and sustainability compliance requirements that add significant costs to their bottom lines. They will also be subject to an increase in operating cost through the banning of many of the methods and chemical inputs currently used. They will see a net reduction in output as a by-product of these changes. It is also possible that an event like COVID-19 could precipitate a collapse of part or all of production, supply and distribution mechanisms.

MICRONUTRIENTS

As we gather more information about just how essential micronutrients are in the form of trace elements and minerals to human health, we will begin to covet their availability to us. Suppose we only review iron deficiency in the global population, as expressed in the disease of anaemia. In that case, we can see some startling realities.

According to the World Health Organization (WHO):

> Anaemia is a condition in which the number of red blood cells or the hemoglobin concentration within them is lower than normal. Hemoglobin is needed to carry oxygen and if you have too few or abnormal red blood cells or not

> enough hemoglobin, there will be a decreased capacity of the blood to carry oxygen to the body's tissues. This results in symptoms such as fatigue, weakness, dizziness and shortness of breath, among others. The optimal hemoglobin concentration needed to meet physiologic needs varies by age, sex, the elevation of residence, smoking habits and pregnancy status. The most common causes of anaemia include nutritional deficiencies, particularly iron deficiency, though deficiencies in folate, vitamins B12 and A are also important causes; hemoglobinopathies; and infectious diseases, such as malaria, tuberculosis, HIV and parasitic infections.[57]

WHO has declared that anaemia is a serious global public health problem and it particularly affects young children and pregnant women. It estimates that 42 per cent of children younger than five years of age and 40 per cent of pregnant women worldwide are anaemic.

The main contributing factor in reducing iron levels and other micronutrients in fresh vegetables is believed to be genetic plant breeding.[58] As farmers and producers have been selectively breeding plants that not only grow faster but also larger, these gains are often made through the overproduction of plant dry matter. Containing only carbohydrates, increases in plant dry matter appear to inversely correlate with the plant's element and mineral uptake. These larger plants may target growth-related nutrients within the soil at the cost of other available minerals and elements.

This kind of genetic breeding also promotes mono-cropping and reduces biodiversity. The loss of diversity in the types and varieties of vegetables we can choose from at our local grocery store also impacts our ability to purchase nutrient-rich foods.

Post-harvest, transportation and storage losses for iron are also impactful. Suppose we imagine a usual situation for a popular iron-rich vegetable like spinach. In that case, we can see that our supermarket purchase decision is based on false, outdated information. In 2019, almost US$400 million of fresh or chilled spinach was exported around the world. The central exporting countries were in Europe followed by the US. If the research data on nutrient loss and, more specifically, iron in plants are correct, then there has been a reduction of up to 40 per cent in the plants' iron levels at harvest compared to 40 years ago. When combined with the significant iron loss during post-harvest processing, transportation and storage,[59] we can see that the often-promoted and community-perceived benefits of eating spinach for increasing our iron intake can be considered misleading.

At a temperature of 22 degrees Celsius, iron levels of the spinach are almost entirely depleted just two days after harvest. This can be extended by up to six to eight days if the spinach is transported and stored at a temperature below 4 degrees Celsius. For international export and supply to occur, to get the 'fresh' spinach to stores for consumers, these timeframes would require high-speed air freight for delivery, adding significantly to the environmental cost.[60]

Iron is only one of the array of micronutrients we need for our bodies to achieve optimal health. Many of the minerals and elements we need are affected by declining levels in pre-harvest fresh produce and post-harvest losses in the same way.

More research is being done to fully understand the importance of micronutrients in our overall health and wellness. We need to realise that current production and supply methods of fresh fruits and vegetables reduce or negate the levels of micronutrients in the products at our local supermarket. In many cases, they are either in amounts that are negligible or frankly not present.

MALNUTRITION

If we move further downstream of the issue of our food and its reduced nutrition levels, we need to also look at global malnutrition. Malnutrition is an obvious precursor to hunger and starvation as a lack of access to quality food will first be presented as an issue of malnutrition.

Endemic malnutrition would logically be an issue of hunger and starvation, or is it?

A 2019 study at the Medical University of Vienna found that:

> Among the great challenges the world faces are how to ensure food security for its growing population – projected to rise to around 10 billion by 2050 – so it can meet their nutritional needs for a healthy life. Current regulations and literature on food security mainly focus on food quantity (i.e., portion sizes), daily calorie intake and methods for increasing food production and too little on food and diet quality and the holistic effects of (mal)nutrition.[61]

The *Lancet* Commission on obesity reviewed hundreds of studies from the last two decades and reported that 'malnutrition in all its forms, including obesity, undernutrition, and other dietary risks, is the leading cause of poor health globally'.[62] In the world, three times more people are suffering from malnutrition and obesity than are suffering from malnutrition and starvation.[63] Sixteen per cent of the global population are considered obese, and by the end of this decade, the US will have almost half of its population categorised as obese.[64] The adoption of highly processed food in Western-style diets that can have extraordinarily little nutritional value and next to no micronutrient density is the single biggest health issue facing humanity and the number-one cause of disease and death in the US.[65]

Let's look at the root cause. We see that red meat consumption is the leading cause of these dietary and health issues and the number-one cause of agricultural-based environmental damage. To add to this, more than 40 per cent of the agricultural land in the US is used for livestock production.[66] The issue is also primarily driven by the fact that healthy food is becoming more expensive as processed food becomes cheaper and cheaper.

As other countries adopt these Western-style diets, they are now counting the public health, environmental and social costs. In China, childhood obesity has risen to 20 per cent from 5 per cent since 1995, and obesity rates have tripled in India in the same period and now affect an incredible 66.8 million people.[67]

The truth is that the issue of starvation and obesity is inextricably linked to malnutrition and undernutrition.

The interplay of the food we eat, our bodies and how they supply the energy and nutrition we need to be 'healthy' is incredibly complex. With the fall in the nutrition of our food, we have seen an incredible rise in the use of supplements to supply the nutrients in which our diets are now deficient. Once again, consumer demand for convenience makes it far easier to take a multivitamin tablet than to make a multivitamin meal, let alone personally grow the food for the multivitamin meal.

Studies show that the use of multivitamin pills and supplements is increasing every year but little if any benefit is derived from their use.[68] Our bodies are finely tuned to break down and process food and manage and measure the vitamins and nutrients in them. The same does not occur when we take a pill or tablet. Often the 'filler' chemicals and compounds in the multivitamins or supplements confuse the body as to whether it is even food.

When we eat a carrot or capsicum, our body can use and absorb the vitamins and minerals available. This happens because of the interplay with different vitamins and minerals present in the food. Researchers are now finding that often the body will not absorb a nutrient without the presence of other, symbiotic nutrients.[69] Our bodies also regulate how much of a vitamin or nutrient is required and will pass through any oversupply. Studies have shown that when we use multivitamins or supplements, the body can pass the entire amount through our system without any positive effect.[70]

The companies that make these multivitamins and supplements are being cryptically honest to consumers by always stating that these products 'cannot be used to replace a healthy balanced diet'. Unfortunately, this is precisely what most consumers believe they do and why they use them. At best, and as research shows,[71] if your body was severely deficient in a vitamin or mineral, then supplements might help bridge a short-term gap until you could improve your diet. At worst, they are merely introducing more potentially harmful chemicals and compounds into your body that are causing far more harm than good, not to mention the economic cost.

Suppose you know of someone with hundreds of dollars in multivitamin supplements in their cupboards. In that case, they should consider creating a Smart Garden that would provide themselves and their environment with infinitely more benefits for less cost. As I repeat many times during this book, the healthiest way you can eat and live is to grow your own food. There is simply no comparison between picking and eating something fresh from your own home garden and either buying a hollow, nutritionally depleted version of it from a supermarket or taking a chemically processed version of it as a tablet. The closer you are to where your food is grown, the healthier you are, the healthier the world is, and the healthier our future becomes.

THE DESTRUCTION OF OUR SOIL

'The nation that destroys its soil destroys itself.'

– Franklin D. Roosevelt, US President, in a 1937 letter to US state governors, warning of the dire situation they faced with the impact of industrial agriculture and climate conditions

Another issue that is affecting our food security is the rapid loss of topsoil around the world. Our topsoil is responsible for more than 95 per cent of our food.[72] Current estimates show that we are losing 30 football fields of topsoil every five seconds.[73] If this rate continues, we will lose all of our topsoils within the next 60 years. Already the loss of healthy topsoil directly impacts more than 3.6 million people globally through hunger and economic hardship.

Around the world, the actual amount of arable farmland is diminishing at an alarming rate. The World Bank claims that only 36.94 per cent of the Earth can be considered 'agricultural' land, and 10.825 per cent is deemed arable.[74] Arable land, by definition, is regarded as being able to be used for large-scale agriculture.

It can take up to 500 years to build a healthy topsoil layer. We have managed to dramatically degrade vast areas of topsoil in less than 100 years of large-scale agriculture. Issues such as soil compaction from large, heavy machinery, nutrient and mineral loss, pesticide and herbicide usage, and wind and rain loss of topsoil due to commercial ploughing and tilling are just a few of the challenges when it comes to large-scale agriculture.

A 2013 study from Cornell University into soil erosion stated:

> Since humans worldwide obtain more than 99.7% of their food (calories) from the land and less than 0.3% from the oceans and aquatic ecosystems, preserving cropland and maintaining soil fertility should be of the highest importance to human welfare. Soil erosion is one of the most serious threats facing world food production. Each year about 10 million ha of cropland are lost due to soil erosion, thus reducing the cropland available for world food production. The loss of cropland is a serious problem because the World Health Organization and the Food and Agricultural Organization report that two-thirds of the world population is malnourished. Overall, the soil is being lost from agricultural areas 10 to 40 times faster than the rate of soil formation imperiling humanity's food security.[75]

The cause of this soil loss is primarily deforestation, population growth, urban expansion, waste and pollution disposal, climate change and destructive farming practices. Deforestation of land to make way for farmland creation is causing untold damage to topsoils in poorer countries. Local populations are forced to clear more and more land to help drive economic growth. Not only is this causing a loss in what was once forest topsoil, but the crops and livestock that are then grown and grazed on the land are generally poor quality. Forest topsoil requires large amounts of added amendments like nutrients and minerals for commercial agriculture. Habitat loss for animals and the destruction of entire ecosystems are another of the many unacceptable deforestation realities.

Population growth and urban expansion are another cause of soil loss. As populations grow and become more urbanised, the pressure to clear more and more land becomes greater. I have seen this first-hand on the outskirts of Sydney, Australia. What were once green farmlands and commercial dairies that I travelled through in my childhood are now vast medium-density housing suburbs containing tens of thousands of homes and related infrastructure. This is being repeated across the globe as populations vie for positions on the city fringe areas.

Heavy industry is also responsible for much of the waste and pollution disposal, which further contributes to topsoil loss through contamination. Heavy metal contamination not only renders any further use of the soil dangerous to human health but, in many cases, those contaminants can take hundreds of years to break down. Often, we are unaware of the levels at which soil contamination has occurred. Numerous news articles have covered stories of families growing fresh produce in the soil of their backyards, only to become severely ill due to the high lead levels found there.[76,77] This is something we will show you how to avoid later in the book in our Smart Garden design.

The financial impact alone of global soil loss has been estimated by *Forbes* magazine to be more than US$8 billion annually.[78] The reality is that topsoil loss is also responsible for biodiversity loss, salinisation and sodification,[79] nutrient imbalance, compaction, sealing, pollution, acidification, erosion and loss of organic carbon matter.

The consequences of global soil loss will lead to issues such as food scarcity, nutrient insecurity, community poverty and social insecurity. Soil loss is just one factor affecting how we currently procure food and sustenance for ourselves and our families. Much of Africa, Asia and some South American and European countries are already experiencing accelerated topsoil loss and erosion that not only needs to be urgently halted but reversed.

The 2019 Global Symposium on Soil Erosion concluded that:

> There is convincing scientific evidence that soil erosion is a global threat to food production systems, available land for future demand, rural livelihoods, human health and biodiversity; and that coordinated effective action needs to be fostered and accelerated to address this issue.[80]

It is hard to imagine that there will not be a significant impact on global agricultural production as the realities of soil erosion become a critical global issue. As crop yields are reduced, water usage needs to increase. The nutritional value of the produce grown in these rapidly disappearing soils is in decline; the cost–benefit equation for all consumers will be paramount.

Even if government mandates were to be passed tomorrow outlawing practices like ploughing and tillage of paddocks, and the use of sloping land for crop production and deforestation, it would take several years, if not many decades, to begin to rebuild even a small part of what has already been lost. As with many of the systemic problems facing food security, media coverage will not highlight the issues until the realities of the damage are felt in the consumer's hip pocket or some environmental catastrophe affects a wealthy community or nation. Unfortunately, the road to any meaningful recovery from soil depletion and loss is an exceptionally long one in human lifetime terms.

A UN report into the Status of the World's Soil Resources[81] showed that the collective impact of water and wind erosion, as a result of unsustainable farming and agricultural activities, could cause a loss of up to 100 tons of soil material per hectare per year, if combined with extreme weather effects, such as those caused by climate change. To put this into perspective, the rate at which topsoil can regenerate through natural processes is approximately only to a depth of 3 centimetres per 1000 years.[82] Therefore, it would take more than 650 years to replace the soil lost from one year of high wind and rainfall occurring on ploughed sloping temperate farmland at the natural rate of soil reproduction and regeneration.

Even today, I can drive around the magnificent farmland of my home state of Tasmania in Australia and see large multi-wheeled tractors tilling and ploughing sloping farmland in preparation for their next crop. An unforeseen weather event such as an extensive rainstorm could have a catastrophic impact on the land if it were to occur before establishing a cover crop.[83] It is my personal belief that no-till farming should be the only method allowed on land that has a greater than 7-degree slope. Agricultural departments within state and federal governments should be addressing these issues today and developing genuinely sustainable soil loss mitigation strategies and compliance frameworks and regulations.

The loss of fertile arable soil needs to be seen in its purest light. It is the loss of the basis of human life and the erosion of not only one of our three most important resources for survival – air, water and soil – but a vital building block to our children's future.

I do not personally believe that the necessary changes will take place until it is far too late. When soil loss mitigation strategies are finally developed, rebuilding programs can eventually be legislated. The method, cost and commercial agriculture function will resemble little of what we see and enjoy today. The rate of global soil depletion and the net effect on the cost and quality of commercial produce is one of the driving reasons behind why my wife and I started our technograrian journey.

SOIL COMPACTION

As the demand to produce more and more food from our farms and agricultural lands grows, so does the need for heavy, large-scale machinery. While this machinery helps with farm efficiency, they do irreparable damage to the precious soil they are harvesting from by way of soil compaction. Soil compaction is when the air in the soil is squeezed out. It is the equivalent of literally squeezing the life out of it. Heavy machinery is not the only cause of soil compaction. Overgrazing of livestock can also cause devastating soil compaction issues.

A 2018 study looked at the effects of soil compaction on crop yields and found:

> Compaction restricts the infiltration of water, increasing runoff and erosion, leading to the loss of valuable nutrients. Soil strength, cone index, bulk density, porosity, moisture content, erosion and runoff, poor plant growth and yields are the major parameters used as indicators of soil compaction. The problems of soil compaction are a global concern. As farmers continue to till the soil for food and fiber production to meet the need of the growing world population, prevention and alleviation practices should be taken into consideration to avoid the negative effects of soil compaction. Farmers are advised to cultivate cover crops; incorporation of organic

matter into the soil; and practicing mixed farming in order to alleviate soil compaction menace.[84]

Not only does soil compaction decrease crop yields and production, but it also assists soil erosion. As part of what is loosely viewed as a much larger 'land degradation syndrome', soil compaction is a problem that already is estimated to affect 4 per cent of the world's landmass.[85] While farmers can help mitigate shallow soil compaction by ripping soil and adding biomass and organic matter, deeper soil compaction presents the most significant issue. Soil can be compacted down to a depth of 1 metre due to the axle weight of the heavy machinery now used in farming. Over the last 20 years, heavy farm machinery's average axle weight has increased from 2 tons to 7 tons. When this type of machinery is used, particularly with wet clay and silt-based soils, deep compaction occurs. They radically affect the water flow and filtering ability of the land and the deep root formation of plants.

Soil compaction lessens the ability of a plant to absorb nutrients as the root growth is restricted, as is water flow. There is less air in the soil to keep microflora and fauna alive, reducing the biological activity in the soil. Soil compaction negatively impacts plant health and resistance to disease and reduces the plant's ability for nutrient uptake. This, of course, becomes another modern agricultural problem that directly affects the nutrient density of the food we consume.

Soil compaction, as with soil erosion, are just two of the factors involved with land degradation. As I have mentioned previously, the amount of arable land we can use for farming and agriculture is shrinking. We need to be aware that at the current rates of land degradation globally, it will be increasingly difficult to feed the global population using current methods and practices with the reduction of natural resources at our disposal. We are at a point in history where a radical change in how we grow and derive our food has become an issue needing emergency attention. Continuation along our current course can only produce an inevitable outcome – a complete collapse in our food system. The destruction of our children's economic, social and environmental futures will be something for which we will all be responsible.

SOIL MICROBIOLOGY

The most fascinating and rewarding aspect of growing food at home during Gemma's and my Smart Garden journey has been soil microbiology. Its direct correlation to having a garden that produces abundant disease-free food is undeniable. What I thought was good soil ten years ago, compared to what I know now, is humbling.

If you want to see the truth of what is the most crucial aspect of a healthy diet, you should get a clean dinner plate and place on it two cups' worth of the soil from which your food is grown.

This is what you are really eating!

Whatever is contained in those cups of soil will have the most significant impact on your health. If it is rich with minerals and nutrients, biological life, decaying organic matter, air and water, then your plants will use all of those elements to be nutrient-packed and disease-free. You can then come along and pick that plant and eat it, and you will, in turn, become nutrient-packed and disease-free. It is a beautiful circular system that is easy to understand and build.

Imagine, though, your food has come from somewhere you have never been. You now have to pour two cups of soil on your dinner plate from some unknown paddock that is perhaps in another country, thousands of kilometres away from you. This is the foundation of what you are eating, and yet you have no idea what it contains. It might be okay. But it could be contaminated and poisoned. It might have next to no nutrients left in it. It might be dead soil with just enough added chemicals to grow some genetically modified plant. These genetically modified plants only require a few base chemicals to grow. They look like a typical plant, except they are sick, so pests attack them, but that problem has been solved because the plant has also been genetically modified to withstand direct spraying of the herbicide glyphosate onto its leaves.

In an article for Northern Australia Land Care Research, Christopher Johns discussed the importance of soil microbiology:

> Soil fertility, or its capacity to enrich natural and agricultural plants, is dependent upon three interacting and mutually dependent components: physical fertility, chemical fertility and biological fertility. Physical fertility refers to the soil's physical properties, including its structure, texture and water absorption and holding capacity, and root penetration. Chemical fertility involves nutrient levels and the presence of chemical conditions such as acidity, alkalinity and salinity that may be harmful or toxic to the plant. Biological fertility refers to the organisms that live in the soil and interact with the other components. These organisms live on soil, organic matter or other soil organisms and perform many vital processes in the soil. Some of them perform critical functions in the nutrient and carbon cycles. Very few soil organisms are pests.
>
> Of the three fertility components, it is the microbiological element, the rich diversity of organisms such as bacteria, viruses, fungi and algae that form interactive microbial communities, that are the most complex and, paradoxically,

> the least well-understood. A near decade-long collaboration between the CSIRO and the Bio-platforms Australia company ranks the understanding of soil microbial communities as important as mapping the galaxies in the universe or the biodiversity of the oceans. It provides an opportunity to discover new species currently unknown to science. Soil microbial communities underpin the productivity of all agricultural enterprises and are primary drivers in ecological processes such as the nutrient and carbon cycling, degradation of contaminants and suppression of soil-borne diseases. They are also intimately involved in a range of beneficial and, at times, essential, interrelationships with plants.[86]

Creating a healthy soil microbiome takes a bit of work. Still, it is critical to growing healthy, nutrient-dense, disease-free produce. With soil degradation happening the world over, we desperately need to start rebuilding the soil microbiome, but the reality of doing this on a large commercial scale presents enormous challenges. Composting your Smart Garden is relatively easy, but composting a couple of hundred or even a couple of thousand acres is infinitely more difficult. Creating healthy soil microbiology is a fundamental, foundational building block for growing healthy produce. It is exceedingly difficult, if not impossible, to do on a vast commercial scale.

DESERTIFICATION

The 2019 United Nations Convention to Combat Desertification found a strong link between land use and drought and the resulting desertification.[87] We need more effective water mitigation strategies and the development of far more green cover programs for land that is already marginal drylands. These drylands already make up approximately 40 per cent of the world landmass. While desertification is a naturally occurring environmental change, it has been accelerated by poor agricultural land use, urbanisation, mining and grazing. This all contributes to soil erosion and a reduction in the ability of the land to retain water.

Water harvesting and capture is the most critical aspect of reversing desertification. As landmasses lose their vegetative cover, the speed of water runoff increases, as does the speed of soil erosion and the leaching of any remaining minerals. Green covers, whether green crops or tree planting programs, help rebuild soil structure and capture some of the rainfall for later use within the plant or crop.

We need to look at land use in these marginal areas with the link between dryland use and drought and desertification. Overgrazing of stock on, and the tillage of, these marginal lands has a disastrous effect. One of the policy frameworks being promoted by the UN and other government agencies is to repurpose the use of this land. Given the opportunity to heal and rebuild, the land can become fertile again. Still, it takes time and a committed response program by authorities.

Drought and desertification affect more than 1.9 billion hectares of land globally and millions of people. Perhaps with government and global NGO support, these marginal dryland agricultural areas could be repurposed from poor agricultural performers to solar energy centres. Ideas like this need to be supported. Up to 50 million people will face displacement from the desertification of their lands by 2050.[88]

When the land becomes desert, the impact it has on the local indigenous populations is devastating. Many are displaced and will move towards city centres to look for employment. Some stay behind, trying to remediate the land and make it fertile once more.

Desertification of our lands is just another unfortunate by-product of our food supply system. We must look at ways to minimise the growth of deserts on our drylands. Indigenous communities need support to create green cover programs that can help stem this growing global issue.

GLOBAL SOIL LOSS

Even though we have only touched on some of the challenges of soil loss and its related causes, we can see the many and varied ways it is occurring. It demonstrates that the soil we rely on for our food is degraded and disappearing at an incredible rate. I believe that this could potentially see humans facing a global starvation crisis within our children's lifetimes. Large-scale agriculture has continued to grow exponentially, driven by the ever-increasing need to feed the world. Still, the actual cost of the damage it has wrought on human health and the environment is only now being fully understood and, indeed, calculated.

If we do not change how we farm and produce food and overhaul the entire global food supply system, we will lose much of what we take for granted today. Clean drinking water, shopping at the local supermarket and enjoying the remaining farmland and forests will soon no longer be available to us. Our soil is a finite resource being degraded and destroyed by a system built around the need to support infinite growth. The finite cannot support the infinite forever. It will run out.

There can be no doubt that most of the damage and destruction that is happening to our soils are of our own doing. Climate change, in large part, is simply an accelerator to a system of destruction that is itself accelerating. As more forests are destroyed to make way for farmland, that new farmland is exposed to weather events such as floods and, in turn, we lose vast amounts of soil. That farmland is then unable to produce crops, so the cycle begins again, and more forests are cut down. This insanity is becoming more frequent, and the scale of destruction much more massive.

In 2019, debris burning from forest clearing in the Amazon delta in South America was visible in satellite images from space. Perhaps we need someone to use those satellites to take more photos of our soils' destruction to show the world's population just how serious this problem is.

One of the enduring images of the effects of climate change is the starving polar bear floating out to sea on an ever-decreasing piece of arctic ice melt. This is an excellent analogy for humanity's situation and our soil. The amount of soil we all currently stand on and rely upon decreases, like the iceberg in the ocean. How long will it be before we all find ourselves trapped like the polar bear?

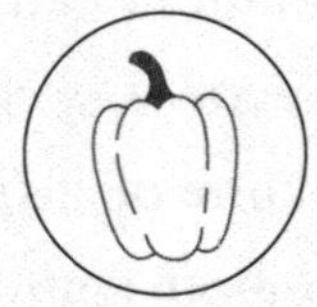

GLOBAL CHEMICAL USE

'The more we pour the big machines, the fuel, the pesticides, the herbicides, the fertilizer and chemicals into farming, the more we knock out the mechanism that made it all work in the first place.'

– David R. Brower, environmentalist who founded several environmental organisations

Fortunately, there is an increase in farmers using no-till methods to produce our food, but changes take time and have a short-term impact on costs and yields. In a research paper for *GM Crops & Food*, agricultural economist Graham Brookes noted that a global ban on glyphosate usage and the planting of genetically modified glyphosate-resistant soybean would see a reduction of up to 85 per cent in the Argentinean soy crop over the first two years of implementation. Glyphosate is now considered by the World Health Organization as a chemical that 'probably causes cancer'.[89]

In his article 'Trends in glyphosate herbicide use in the United States and globally', in 2016, Charles Benbrook wrote:

> Since 1974 in the U.S., over 1.6 billion kilograms of glyphosate active ingredients have been applied, or 19% of the estimated global use of glyphosate (8.6 billion kilograms). Globally, glyphosate use has risen almost 15-fold since the so-called 'Roundup Ready,' genetically engineered glyphosate-tolerant crops were introduced in 1996. Two-thirds of the total volume of glyphosate applied in the U.S. from 1974 to 2014 has been sprayed in just the last 10 years.[90]

The many problems that large-scale agriculture presents to the world, including its negative impacts on the environment, soil quality and human health, will ultimately need a solution. It is reasonable to expect that mandated changes will soon be demanded by the population and governments. As with the research cited above concerning just one issue, such as global glyphosate usage, a ban would see a radical reduction in the production of many core crops such as soy and corn. The economic fallout would be significant. It would impact a vast range of downstream grocery items that rely on soy and corn for raw materials and by-products like corn syrup.

The volume of chemicals used in commercial food production is simply staggering. The largest group are called 'organophosphates'.[91] Thirty-six of these are currently approved for use in agriculture in the US, all of which are toxic to humans with varying degrees of exposure.[92] These chemicals not only present a clear and present danger to the health and wellbeing of the human population, as shown through numerous studies, but they also cause untold environmental damage.

In its branded 'Roundup' form, glyphosate was recently the subject of a landmark court case with a couple who successfully won an appeal against the Bayer corporation for damages. The couple were awarded more than US$2 billion after the jury found in favour of their claim that the popular Roundup herbicide product was a contributing factor in the couple's cancer diagnoses.

An excerpt from a news article from the ABC stated:

> The couple's lawyer Brent Wisner said there would be more cases against the company. 'This is not the end, this is the beginning, there are tens of thousands of people out there, probably 30,000, or 40,000 people out there,' he said. 'And I've told Bayer and Monsanto we are coming after them.' German company Bayer bought Monsanto in a $62.5 billion deal last year and is now responsible for the pay-outs against them.[93]

When we consider that approximately 8.6 billion kilograms of glyphosate have been used worldwide since 1974,[94] it is hard to truly understand the health and environmental damage this one chemical has potentially caused. With the prospect of far more lawsuits and the further uncovering of the truths behind glyphosate usage, it is difficult to imagine that its use will be allowed to continue for much longer. As stated above, the Bayer corporation recently purchased the chemical division responsible for the Roundup range of products from Monsanto. I do not believe it will be able to afford the related court payouts from the other unsuccessful legal defences of these products in the future.

Unlike my feeling around the lack of timely response to global soil erosion from government and industry authorities, I believe that continued chemical use in food production will decrease rapidly over the next five to ten years. These successful court cases hit corporate profits in ways that cannot quickly be alleviated. I know that large grocery buying groups are incredibly aware that they too could become targeted in civil suits should the general public realise they have been fed a chemical cocktail via their fruit and vegetable section for decades.

Like many people, I see this ultimately leading to a push for more chemical-free and organically grown products. That will lead to a significant loss of yield as organic agriculture does not produce the food volume that artificial chemicals have allowed conventional farmers to produce. I appreciate that many organic growers and supporters might want to challenge this assumption. Any research into conventional versus organic crop production will support these findings. The analogy that best describes the difference between the output of chemical versus non-chemical agriculture would be expecting a chemical-free weightlifter to lift the same weights as one taking a lifetime of anabolic steroids.

This reduction in output would mean potentially higher prices for consumers based on simple supply and demand models. Another issue with this reduction in supply will be the pressure that corporate grocery buyers can exert on producers to meet supply requirements and the corruption that can occur when a farmer's livelihood is placed in jeopardy. To say the grocery buyers play hardball with producers is something of an understatement. The realities of these pressures have already caused unscrupulous use of the term 'organic' by producers[95] and supermarkets that have made their way into news headlines. Organic farmers need significant support and representation from industry bodies and for them to act not only as regulators but also intermediaries with buying groups.

For example, Australian organic certification bodies are many and varied, as are the standards and requirements they each promote. The formation of a single national organic certification body would appear to be a logical step towards a stronger, more cohesive and supportive industry. Regrettably, many of the current organic certification bodies still suffer from infighting and finger-pointing while trying to achieve great things. It may take government oversight of the organic industry and certification requirements before consumers can genuinely trust organic claims made by producers.

The historical use of pesticides and herbicides has already caused so much injury and harm to people and the planet. We are slowly becoming much more conscious of the urgent need to stop their use. Unfortunately, new and novel chemicals are becoming routine in our food production systems to fight bacteria like *E. coli*. We are far more likely to become sick from salmonella and listeria from fruit and vegetables than the bioaccumulation effect of pesticides and herbicides in our systems.

Bacteria like salmonella and listeria are promoted when leaf tissue is cut, as in the ready-to-eat salad packets we find in our grocery store today. To combat this, producers are now using chlorinated sprays and washes to help kill and remove any potential bacterial contamination during packaging. While many of us have daily exposure to chlorine[96] as it is used extensively as an additive to urban water supplies, it is shown that the currently known side effects of exposure can include: airway irritation, wheezing, difficulty breathing, sore throat, cough, chest tightness, eye irritation and skin irritation. I am not a doctor and don't have any medical experience, but that does not sound like the human body is comfortable with being exposed to chlorine. Perhaps in another ten years, we will be able to delete Roundup from the court report above and replace it with chlorine?

While I am only touching on just a couple of essential issues related to chemicals found in our food supply chain, the regrettable reality is the list of chemicals used is extraordinarily long. Research into what the actual costs are to human and environmental health is minimal. For the most part, we do not know. It is tough to find accurate information from reliable sources because there are ultimately billions of dollars at stake and veils of secrecy and industrial malfeasance.

The one thing I do know is that if you grow your own fruits and vegetables at home, the levels of toxins and chemicals you and your family will be exposed to will be far, far less than by purchasing food from your supermarket.

It ultimately depends on what you believe and what is important to you.

SOIL FERTILITY

Many of the chemicals in industrial agriculture are used to improve soil fertility and increase crop yields, but many, such as herbicides or the chemicals used to kill weeds and reduce plant disease, impair soil fertility and reduce a plant's ability to uptake nutrients. Modern farming is faced with a never-ending dilemma: increasing the use of inorganic fertilisers to combat the reduction in soil fertility and plant growth created in part by the use of herbicides that, in turn, reduce the effectiveness of fertilisers to improve soil fertility. The use of these chemicals causes enormous environmental damage. When we include the negative impacts of pesticide use and the genetic modification of plant crops, in some cases with the DNA of animals, it is not hard to understand why the current industrial farming model is unsustainable, even in the short-term.

With this in mind, the agrochemical industry is still set to grow at around 3.6 per cent per year and be worth an estimated US$246 billion by 2025.[97] It is interesting to note that the global loss of arable farmland is currently projected at 3.4 per cent per year[98], which is remarkably close to the growth in agrochemical use. Current estimates show that our global use of nitrogen-based agrochemicals is more than 106,000 kilotonnes per annum. Of that, 56 per cent of the consumption and use is in the Asia–Pacific region, with China being the most significant user. The use of these chemicals has led to an increased crop volume, viewed by the industry as an efficiency improvement.[99] The metrics used to calculate an on-farm efficiency improvement do not consider things like the natural capital cost (environmental damage) and social and health costs (increasing cancer rates, poverty, etc.).

The *International Journal of Low-Carbon Technologies* reported in 2018:

> In most developing countries, the pollution caused by agricultural chemicals is even more serious. The usage volume of fertilizers and pesticides in China has been recorded as the highest in the world. Specifically, its chemical fertilizer usage volume has reached more than 59 million tons and pesticide more than 1.8 million tons. Alarmingly, the total utilization rate of fertilizers and pesticides is only 35%, and thus, any fertilizer and pesticide losses are likely to contaminate soil, surface water and groundwater. In China, estimates indicate that contaminated arable land area is 150 million acres, accounting for 8.3% of the total arable land in the nation. Also, nearly half of the groundwater resources have been inordinately polluted by agricultural chemicals, which seriously threaten the safety of drinking water in China, especially in rural areas . . . The consequences of increased use of agricultural chemicals transcend the environment. Farmers in developing countries are experiencing, either short-term or long-term, health effects from exposures to agricultural chemicals, including severe symptoms (e.g. headaches, skin rashes, eye irritations) and some chronic effects (e.g. cancer, endocrine disruption, birth defects).[100]

The real growth drivers in the use of these agrochemicals are developing nations. Many of these countries are trying to improve crop volume yields and on-farm efficiencies without any oversight or complete understanding of the drastically negative consequences of the unchecked use of chemicals. They negatively affect both the land they are used upon and the health of consumers who purchase the produce grown with them. Like the US and China, some countries are creating policies around the continued use of specific chemical categories, having recognised that 'the excessive and unsystematic application of agrichemical inputs, pesticides and fertilizers, in particular, is an obstacle to the development of sustainable agriculture, and poses a threat to the environment and humans alike'.[101]

We need to urgently address the issue of chemicals in all aspects of agriculture. With the rise of the chemical industry in the 1950s, many chemicals have never been thoroughly analysed to look at their human and environmental impact. The reality is that many of these chemicals can last for several lifetimes in the environment and, perhaps more concerningly, inside our bodies. Due to the assumed complexity surrounding proper analysis and research, many chemical producers are self-regulating their billion-dollar corporations. Like the recent civil suit involving glyphosate usage, I believe we will see many, many similar court actions against these companies in the future.

CHEMICAL RUNOFF

The excessive use of fertilisers is another consequence of our current agricultural practices. Not only is the use of organic and inorganic fertilisers contaminating our waterways, but it is also producing vast amounts of greenhouse gases. Fertiliser runoff is creating massive dead zones in our rivers, lakes and oceans. There are currently more than 400 of these aquatic dead zones worldwide.[102] Dead zones occur because of several factors, but the main contributing factor is fertiliser runoff from industrial agriculture. There has been an explosion in the use of nitrogen, phosphorus and potassium in industrial agriculture over the last 120 years. As the chemicals break down, they produce nitrates and phosphates.

When they end up in our waterways, fertilisers promote a surge in algae growth; they are, after all, 'plant growth promoters'. These algal blooms, as they are called, choke our waterways. The process is called 'eutrophication', which describes how our waterways become enriched with these nutrients and chemicals and cause aquatic plant life to grow at unnatural levels. This, in turn, creates what scientists call a hypoxic zone. This describes an area with all the oxygen removed from the water, making it impossible for air-breathing aquatic life to survive.[103] One of the largest of these dead zones is in the Gulf of Mexico and affects almost 8000 square kilometres.

All marine life in the area is either suffocated and dies or moves on to a new location. Local ecosystems are destroyed and are failing to rebuild and return in many cases. Not only do these algal blooms remove all the oxygen in the water, they are also highly toxic to human beings. One hazardous variety of algae is cyanobacteria or blue-green algae, as it is commonly referred to. It is poisonous to humans and animals from either contact or accidental consumption. Large blue-green algal blooms are occurring worldwide, and their incidence is growing at an alarming rate.

Fertiliser runoff is now believed to have contaminated drinking water with nitrates and nitrites. The use of nitrogen fertiliser on farms results in excess nitrates and nitrites making their way into underground aquifers and drinking wells. Nitrates are essential to human health and are naturally occurring in many foods like beetroot and spinach. The issues arise when we are exposed to excessive amounts of them through contaminated food and water. Poisoning from nitrates causes a condition called methemoglobinemia. Nitrates are converted into nitrites in our mouths, stomach and intestines. These nitrites oxidise iron in red blood cells and impair their ability to carry oxygen. When humans have been exposed to these nitrites' toxic level, the symptoms include difficulty breathing, headaches, nausea and a bluish tint to their skin.[104]

An updated study published in 2018 in the *Environmental Research and Public Health Journal* stated:

> Nitrate levels in our water resources have increased in many areas of the world largely due to applications of inorganic fertilizer and animal manure in agricultural areas. The regulatory limit for nitrate in public drinking water supplies was set to protect against infant methemoglobinemia, but other health effects were not considered.
>
> The risk of specific cancers and congenital disabilities may be increased when nitrate is ingested under conditions that increase the formation of N-nitroso compounds. We previously reviewed epidemiologic studies before 2005 of nitrate intake from drinking water and cancer, adverse reproductive outcomes and other health effects. Since that review, more than 30 epidemiologic studies have evaluated drinking water nitrate and these outcomes.
>
> The most common endpoints studied were colorectal cancer, bladder, and breast cancer (three studies each), and thyroid disease (four studies). Considering all studies, the strongest evidence for a relationship between drinking water nitrate ingestion and adverse health outcomes (besides methemoglobinemia) is for colorectal cancer, thyroid disease,

and neural tube defects. Many studies observed increased risk with ingestion of water nitrate levels that were below regulatory limits.[105]

OCEAN IMPACT

The aquatic dead zone in the Gulf of Mexico is one of the world's largest and has been created by agrochemical runoff. Though the area affected does change yearly, depending on environmental conditions such as winds and tides, it consistently grows. In 1997 the Hypoxia Task Force was set up in the US to reduce the total affected area to 5000 square kilometres by 2015. In 2015 the area affected was almost three times that size, and the date to achieve the target area size was then reset to 2035.

The gulf area is now suffering from more than 50 years of agrochemical runoff, particularly nitrogen runoff. Scientists believe that if all agricultural chemical runoff into the waterway were to stop immediately, it would still take at least another 30 years for the area to make a significant recovery. Government departments are trying to achieve a 20 per cent reduction in the level of chemical runoff entering the gulf, but are finding that even achieving this modest target is difficult.

An article in *The Guardian* in 2018 warned:

> The ailing Gulf of Mexico is emblematic of global suffocation of the oceans caused by modern agriculture, sewage and climate change, which is causing waters to warm and hold less oxygen. At least 500 sites experiencing hypoxia, or oxygen deprivation, have been reported near coasts worldwide, up from just 50 in 1950. The true number may be much higher, experts believe.[106]

While some scientists and associated government departments are now acting to stem the amount of chemicals that make their way into waterways, most efforts are directed at giving farmers grants and subsidies to assist in runoff mitigation. These financial incentives are often redirected and do extraordinarily little in creating actual change to the main underlying assumptions and behaviours that drive on-farm chemical use and the level of runoff.[107,108]

Chemical use in our food production system has grown to a level where our continued ignorance and inaction will only lead to the systematic destruction of the environment and our health. It is the by-product of the inherent evil that exists with large corporations and their drive to profits. As with plastic pollution that we covered earlier in the book, I believe that any product produced that has a net negative impact on the environment and our health needs to be taxed out of existence. It currently presents as the only motivation that would drive companies and corporations to do the research required to find alternative products or methods. A tax would also supply governments with the funding to begin programs to support the people and environments that have been affected and, in some cases, destroyed by these chemical products. Litigation will also help drive change, but often the payouts made by these businesses represent a small fraction of their operating profit.

Ultimately, as individuals and consumers, we must be much more active in not supporting the things we now know are destroying what little is left as our legacy for our children. As a parent who is aware of these things, I know that assessing what is and what is not of concern is challenging. Often, the real facts and information are difficult, if not impossible, to wade through in our attempt to make more informed purchase decisions. That is why I believe we need to create more of our own food and produce. Our addiction to convenience must at some point be overtaken by our greater responsibility to the safety and future of ourselves and our family.

CLIMATE WARMING

'We have to change how we produce and consume food, not just for environmental reasons, but because this is an existential issue for humans.'

–Janet Ranganathan, Vice President for Research, Data, and Innovation at the World Resources Institute

As climate change impacts are felt more and more worldwide, the consequences will undoubtedly affect our ability to access food at the prices and levels of supply that we have historically enjoyed. Natural weather events are becoming more extreme, and records are being reset continuously for the longest drought, largest flood, highest wind or heaviest rain. These extreme weather events are already having devastating ramifications on crop production around the globe. Corn, soy and wheat are staple ingredients for a vast range of processed food products and production outputs have been significantly reduced in areas affected by prolonged drought.

Let's look at droughts over the last 20 years in places like South America, the US and Australia. It is obvious their duration, severity and regularity are all increasing from historical averages. We see severe droughts being classed as one in 100-year events, but these are happening with far greater frequency. The drought in southern Australia at the beginning of the new millennium was considered by many as a one in 1000-year drought. It was undoubtedly the worst recorded since European settlement more than 200 years ago.

The consequences of these events cannot be overstated. Farmers cannot withstand the economic impact of a total loss of income over multiple years. Many farmers have already faced bankruptcy and moved from the land to urban areas for employment. We already see that the net result of this loss of agricultural productivity is the inevitable price increase for essential commodities and the non-availability of products once in full supply. Prices can quickly quadruple if we face severe shortages.

Drought impact is measured by years and severity. These timeframes often allow farmers to employ some level of mitigation, such as shipping in water or adjusting to more drought-resistant varieties for their crops. However, many weather events can be equally devastating and occur over a few short days. Yet their aftermath is felt for many years. After Cyclone Larry in 2006 in northern Australia, banana prices quickly went from $2.50 per kilogram to $15 per kilogram. More than 80 per cent of the region's banana production had been destroyed. This weather event was followed by a similar event when Cyclone Yasi occurred in 2011, just five years later.

A study by the University of Reading, 'Impact of Climate Change on Agriculture', in 2019, found:

> Climate change is likely to contribute substantially to food insecurity in the future by increasing food prices and reducing food production. Food may become more expensive as climate change mitigation efforts increase energy prices.

> Water required for food production may become scarcer due to increased crop water use and drought. Competition for land may increase as certain areas become climatically unsuitable for production. Besides, extreme weather events associated with climate change may cause sudden reductions in agricultural productivity, leading to rapid price increases. For example, heatwaves in the summer of 2010 led to yield losses in key production areas, including Russia, Ukraine and Kazakhstan, and contributed to a dramatic increase in the price of staple foods. These rising prices forced growing numbers of local people into poverty, providing a sobering demonstration of how the influence of climate change can result in food insecurity.[109]

In Europe, the European Environmental Agency (EEA) has already flagged many concerns for its agricultural sector due to the impact of climate change. In their report from April 2019, one of the critical issues facing the sector concerning climate change is that it is responsible for much of the emissions that are accelerating the atmosphere's warming. It noted that the agricultural industry was the most significant contributor to non-CO_2 greenhouse gas (GHG) emissions:

> The (agricultural) sector accounts for around 10% of all GHGs in the EU. Non-CO_2 emissions of methane (CH_4) emissions from enteric fermentation make up the largest share (38%) of all GHG emissions in the sector. Emissions from the use of fertilisers, manure storage and livestock need to be reduced, which depends on the effectiveness of implementing key relevant EU policies.[110]

The reality of this situation is that if current climate changes continue and possibly accelerate, the EEA forecasts a 16 per cent reduction in economic activity in the European agricultural industry by 2050. With growing populations within the EU and increased demand, this reduction will directly impact prices and availability. Suppose the EEA can implement the changes and regulations required to reduce emissions from the agricultural sector? In that case, the loss of economic activity could be equal to or higher than that 16 per cent reduction in economic activity.[111] Many current agricultural practices will see a marked decrease in yields and productivity as they struggle to adopt more sustainable industrial practices.

Climate change is just another major factor that exposes our global food security to risk. As we understand the ramifications of global warming entirely and its direct impact on the causation of extreme weather events, the opportunity for unforeseen and catastrophic implications to agriculture is further highlighted. As with any complex system of dependent and interrelated parts, it only requires a slight change in one part of the system to impact and possibly collapse the system as a whole.

Perhaps this recent warning from the United Nations Intergovernmental Report on Climate Change best sums up our current situation:

> Humans must drastically alter food production to prevent the most catastrophic effects of global warming.[112]

ISOLATED WEATHER EVENTS

The impact of isolated weather events can create a supply shock that quickly drives prices much higher for certain foods and leaves supermarket shelves empty. With the increasing severity of weather events like droughts and floods, their potential impact on the agricultural sector could be devastating.

Research shows that of all the natural weather events that affect arable farmland, drought and floods are responsible for 80 per cent of what is deemed a catastrophic event.[113] These events are growing in regularity and scale with every decade. Without active programs around reducing the effects of land change and greenhouse gas emissions, the affected area and size of farmland will continue to grow. It is widely accepted that global food production needs to increase by 70 per cent from current levels to feed the global population by 2050.[114] It is hard to imagine that this increase will not have substantial economic impacts, not only to the affected regions and countries but also to the countries that rely on importing food from these areas.

Droughts can leave affected areas more prone to desertification and reduce once arable farmland to a wasteland of soil erosion and baked earth. Floods can move thousands of tons of fertile topsoil into our rivers and oceans, rendering productive land a hollow shell of its former self. We currently have no way of rebuilding these vast areas back into arable farmland. Once destroyed, they will remain so until the natural environment can start rebuilding, which will take several generations even with human interventions and support.

Warming atmospheric and ocean temperature, deforestation, urban land use, chemical use, and the current production methods used to create our food, particularly livestock production, are critical components in worsening drought and flood events.

In 2021, ScienceDaily.com reported, 'More and more rainfall extremes are observed in regions around the globe – triggering both wet and dry records.' It found that there are significant differences between regions: 'The central and Eastern US, northern Europe and northern Asia have experienced heavy rainfall events that have led to severe floods in the recent past. In contrast, most African regions have seen an increased frequency of months with a lack of rain.' One particular study, the first to systematically analyse and quantify changes in record-breaking monthly rainfall events from all over the globe, was based on data from roughly 50,000 weather stations worldwide. It stated: 'Climate change from fossil fuel greenhouse gases has long been expected to disturb rainfall patterns.[115]

Although just another aspect of the universal risks faced by our food production system, weather events like droughts and floods that are increasing in length and severity will cause an intensification in the number of people suffering from starvation and malnutrition. Based on recently revised data, droughts are responsible for more than half of the deaths attributed to natural disasters.[116] Governments are struggling to meet the needs of feeding mass populations without the economic resources to import food.

In 2019 Ibrahim Thaiw, the executive secretary for the UN Convention to Combat Desertification (UNCCD), stated:

> We are fast running out of time to build our resilience to climate change, avoid the loss of biological diversity and valuable ecosystems and achieve all other Sustainable Development Goals, but we can turn around the lives of the over 3.2 billion people all over the world that are negatively impacted by desertification and drought if there is political will. And we can revitalise ecosystems that are collapsing from a long history of land transformation and, in too many cases, unsustainable land management.[117]

We need to develop land restoration programs to reverse the damage to land already affected by drought and flood degradation.

The UNCCD warns that, 'Droughts are getting worse.' It estimates that by 2025, some 1.8 billion people will experience severe water shortages, and two-thirds of the world's population will be living in 'water-stressed' conditions. Droughts, though complex and slow to develop, cause more deaths than other types of disasters, and the UNCCD predicts that by 2045, droughts will have forced as many as 135 million people from their homes.[118]

On 17 July 2020, the famous tea-growing area of Assam in India experienced an entire year's worth of rainfall in just one day. The resultant flooding impacted more than 3.5 million people and affected 100,000 hectares of farmland and crops.[119]

Catastrophic events like these are happening across the globe. Still, with the media's fixation on politics and celebrity, we hear little if anything about them.

In all likelihood, the first we will know of these events is when we make an inquiry to our local supermarket chain store as to why they do not have certain items we want to purchase. They will probably let us know that the entire annual production of Product X has been destroyed due to an extreme weather event, but the supermarket has secured a new supplier, and new Product X arrives in a couple of weeks. Of course, they're unlikely to also mention that new Product X will be three times the price.

PESTILENCE

Climate change will also affect plant health, disease and pestilence. Recently, we've seen unprecedented locust swarms in both Africa and South America. Keith Cressman from the FAO[120] believes that these devastating locust plagues are a direct consequence of climate change. In an article in *National Geographic*, he noted that as cyclones on the coast of Africa push inland with greater intensity due to rising ocean temperatures, vast areas of inland arid regions are turned into lakes and provide an ideal environment for the locust swarms to develop.[121]

The impact of locust swarms is disastrous for local farmers. The swarms can consume the vast majority of crops and produce as they move across the landscape. More than 13 million people faced acute food shortages in Djibouti, Eritrea, Ethiopia, Kenya and Somalia, with an estimated further 20 million on the brink.[122] The 2019 climate conditions off the Arabian Peninsula were considered extreme by any measure and shattered many records. It included the most hurricane days recorded and the most 'accumulated cyclone energy' ever measured. The rare December storm that is believed to have triggered the locust outbreak was just one symptom.

The World Bank produced a fact sheet on the damage and associated costs of the outbreak in Africa:

> The outbreak is evolving quickly. As of mid-April 2020, 23 countries have been affected: 9 in the wider East Africa region, 11 in North Africa & the Middle East, and 3 in South Asia. A recent joint impact assessment report by the Government of Ethiopia and FAO estimates that the desert locust outbreak in Ethiopia alone has caused 356,286 metric tons of cereal loss, along with the destruction of 197,163 ha of cropland and 1,350,000 ha of pasturelands, with more than 1 million Ethiopians in need of food assistance as result.[123]

When writing this book, another locust swarm was also affecting Argentina and Brazil in South America. It currently measures 6 square kilometres in size and is estimated to contain more than 40 million locusts. There are also new locust outbreaks affecting Pakistan and parts of Asia. The total economic cost for these global outbreaks is forecast to be in the tens, if not hundreds, of billions. Not only are these countries experiencing the effects of these unprecedented locust plagues, but they are also in the grip of the

COVID-19 pandemic, with several of the countries suffering from high infection and mortality rates.

This 'perfect storm' of pestilence and pandemic will undoubtedly have an immensely negative impact on the sovereign food security of these countries. The longer-term global impact could mirror the food shortages of 2007–08. We could rapidly be facing catastrophic increases in international starvation rates and see a pronounced uptick in global inflation, particularly for foods like cereals and grains.

With governments already struggling to deal with the massive loss of economic productivity due to the COVID-19 pandemic, mandated lockdowns and increased costs of associated public health support, perhaps the added burden of these future locust outbreaks will be enough to potentially bankrupt many nations already struggling under unprecedented challenges.

THE CHANGE IN CLIMATE CHANGE

The effects of climate change will be many and far-reaching. We are only beginning to understand the actual human and economic costs of the increased severity of events like droughts, floods and pest outbreaks. We will see the direct impact of these and other climate change realities in the decreasing food security levels that we once took for granted. These will be first felt in developing countries but will ultimately impact the world as a whole. These impacts will manifest themselves in a net reduction in agricultural output and, ultimately, higher prices and decreasing nutritional quality for consumers.

Dietary changes will be either economically forced upon us or potentially mandated by governments struggling to feed populations under increased production and supply pressure.

Cuba faced a unique set of circumstances after the Cuban Missile Crisis of the 1960s. They were forced to become predominantly self-sufficient as a nation and unable to rely on imported oil and products. They implemented government-mandated national food handouts that focused on minimum productive nutrition levels for their people.[124] This caused an explosion in organic farming and the implementation of self-sufficient personal policies. Vegetable gardens appeared everywhere, on rooftops, balconies and in parking lots. Farmers with the knowledge of how to grow food became the prized professionals of their communities. The country decentralised from their cities and moved back to rural and agrarian communities.

Though the nuanced factors for the changes in Cuba do not precisely mirror what is happening in the world today concerning climate change, I believe many of the policies that have proven so effective in Cuba will have to be implemented in many other countries. Large-scale industrial agriculture places all a nation's eggs in one basket, so to speak, by centralising food supply. If these nations then experience events like these climate-driven locust plagues that destroy their food production capacity, the country will have fewer options to fulfil potentially basic community food requirements.

PREDICTING THE FUTURE

'We do not inherit the earth from our ancestors, we borrow it from our children.'

– Native American proverb

In the preceding chapters, we have touched on only some of the issues currently affecting our future food security. There are many more we have not covered. Much more research is needed into what is occurring and how there is a genuine potential for a systemic breakdown or total collapse.

I want to highlight that we are in a period of rapid and radical change in how we access healthy, nutritious food for ourselves and our families. We need to take far more responsibility for the environmental and social impacts of obtaining our food. Supporting systems that cause harm to human health and the destruction of the environment must be urgently reconsidered.

Many aspects of the way large-scale food production and distribution are currently carried out are at risk and desperately need to be changed and overhauled. It is time our continued total reliance on, and support of, our current methods must be deeply questioned. Our tacit approval of how food is grown, processed and distributed needs to be framed in the truth. Realities of falling nutritional quality, toxic chemical exposure, and massive environmental and ecological damage are only part of the problems.

We undeniably face a high degree of uncertainty when it comes to our future. We have fallen into the trap of complacency, as we have lived through the most significant period of advancement and growth in the history of humanity. History shows us that the level of stability we have enjoyed in the developed world is not the norm. Significant periods of upheaval and change are a natural part of human development cycles.

These are also issues brought to greater public attention by a new generation of politicians and policymakers. The way we access our food, the quality that we demand and the sustainability of its production will change radically over the next decade.

These changes will be both consumer and politically led.

Now is the time to fortify your ability to access healthy fresh produce and create a living insurance policy around the food you eat. Often, as I have stated before, finding simple solutions to complex problems is difficult, if not usually impossible. Your Smart Garden is a simple solution to a vast array of complex issues facing the world. By reducing our participation and reliance upon the system, we begin to make the changes we need, one garden at a time.

PART TWO

THE SMART GARDEN BENEFITS

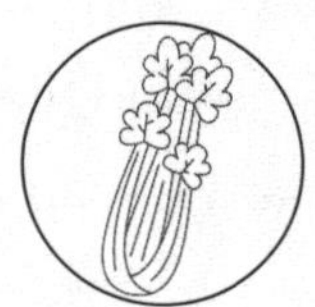

HOMEGROWN REWARDS

'Start with the belief that your life can indeed be changed, and that you have the power to change it.'

– George Bernard Shaw, playright, critic, polemicist and political activist

Let us now look at some of the direct benefits we receive by taking the responsibility of growing food in our own homes and communities. I have listed some of the most obvious ones in the following chapters, but the full list of benefits would be much longer with more research.

We all have become more aware of our need to be much healthier and drastically reduce our personal impact on the environment. A Smart Garden can help you make progress towards these outcomes in a simple and achievable way.

Most of us are suffering from some degree of information overload. Research shows we are bombarded with information from news reports and social media about the world's problems. Knowing that we can do something in a simple, actionable way presents us with a solution to address some of these problems. It is a solution that allows us to become better stewards of our precious Earth and help rebuild connections to the community.

Such a simple solution can sound like it must be too good to be true. The straight facts are that you can achieve all these things and more by creating and enjoying a Smart Garden. If you follow our technograrian garden principles, it will be easier and more rewarding than you imagine.

Having a Smart Garden is not complicated or expensive, especially if you compare it to the costs we will all pay if any of the scenarios we have discussed earlier in the book come to fruition.

Let us take a look at some of the benefits your Smart Garden can give you.

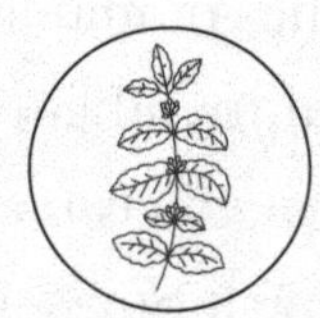

A HEALTHIER YOU

'The doctor of the future will no longer treat the human frame with drugs, but rather will cure and prevent disease with nutrition.'

– Thomas A. Edison in 1903, apparently driven by his concern about the direction that medical science was taking at the time

It is hard to find anyone who does not recognise the importance of being healthier. Our body is an energy system. It needs fuel in the way of food to survive and do the things our minds want it to do. The quality of that fuel directly and profoundly affects the performance of our bodies. The better the input, the better the output . . . simple!

But what real impact does better fuel (our food) have on our bodies?

According to a study by Harvard Medical School:

> To maintain your brain, muscle, bone, nerves, skin, blood circulation, and immune system, your body requires a steady supply of many different raw materials – both macronutrients and micronutrients. You need large amounts of

> macronutrients – proteins, fats, and carbohydrates. And while you only need a small number of micronutrients – vitamins and minerals – failing to get even those small quantities virtually guarantees disease.[125]

Too much of what is promoted today as a 'healthy alternative' is not. How marketers and companies can promote highly processed, sugar- and chemical-filled products as healthy has always been a head-scratcher for me. Eating high-energy protein bars or drinking supplement shakes is considered by many as a healthy thing to do. While these products could be healthier than a product that can make no such claims, we need to understand the difference between healthier and healthy.

If we found ourselves bedridden due to chronic malnutrition and ate a packet of organic high-protein muesli bars, which gave us enough energy to go for a walk, we would consider ourselves healthier than we were.

But would we now be healthy? Not by a long shot.

If the billions of dollars spent on diet fads, specialty health products, gym memberships and so on were spent building Smart Gardens, we could quickly and easily create healthy communities instead of just healthier ones. Being healthier is an improvement by degrees. In the context of current human health, and considering that half of the world's population will be classified as obese by 2035, is it enough to see a minor improvement from a baseline of incredibly unhealthy?

A positive quantum shift in your personal health would require no more time and effort than an average weekly gym plan and would cost about the same. Not only would you be just as active with a garden, but you would save money as well, and a garden provides something a gym cannot . . . healthy food inputs.

Being able to harvest and then immediately consume fresh, organically grown vegetables and salads is simply without a mass-produced peer. Nothing is more nutritious than being able to pick and eat something. How could any supermarket produce even come close?

Creating your Smart Garden with its enriched soils and an abundance of nutrients and minerals will allow you to grow super-healthy, nutrient-dense food. The produce you grow in your garden will contain the micronutrients that science has shown are crucial to realising our full human health potential. A Smart Garden also means you can consume the produce within minutes of harvesting it, and while all the macronutrients and micronutrients are at their peak. You will be obtaining 100 per cent of the health benefits available to you via your fresh produce.

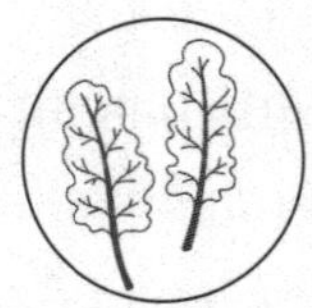

NUTRITION MISSION

'You cannot achieve environmental security and human development without addressing the basic issues of health and nutrition.'

– Gro Harlem Brundtland, former prime minister of Norway, in a 1987 report for the World Commission on Environment and Development, of which she was Chair

Picking whole fresh beetroot from your garden and making a green juice from it will give your body an infusion of vitamins and minerals that no tablet supplement could even closely replicate. The beneficial living enzymes that you will be consuming will help your body break down everything it needs. Amazingly, the vegetables you eat will contain the enzymes you need to fully digest all the sub-components of that particular plant!

Enzymes are a type of protein found in cells. They are responsible for creating and controlling chemical reactions in the body. Enzymes perform critical processes in your body, like building muscle, breaking down the vitamin and mineral components of the food you eat, and destroying toxins. Enzymes are fragile, though, and any form of processing or heating destroys them. It is a requirement by governments and regulators that many foods need to be heat-treated or irradiated before they can be sold to consumers. These processes are used to kill any living material in foods that could be potentially harmful to consumers, like bacteria and moulds. Unfortunately, these processes also kill all beneficial living material, like enzymes, as well.

Enzyme production within our bodies decreases when we get older. As enzymes are directly linked to our metabolism, a lack of enzymes will affect our energy levels. Eating a varied diet of fresh fruits and vegetables is the best way to make sure your body can access an array of these beneficial enzymes.

As we have covered earlier in the book, the nutrition levels of vegetables that are commercially produced have declined over the last 50 years. Much of the nutrition research is focused on protein levels. Still, we need a vast array of vitamins, minerals and other elements to supplement these proteins. These offer us not only better health but also act as a barrier to cancer and disease.

Of the 60 trace elements we find in our body, we only have research data on some of them.

Below is a list of these elements compiled by scientist Micheal Schirber,[126] outlining the percentage contained in our bodies and what deficiency in them could mean to our health:

> **Nitrogen** (3%) is found in many organic molecules, including the amino acids that make up proteins and the nucleic acids that make up DNA.
>
> **Calcium** (1.5%) is the most common mineral in the human body – nearly all of it found in bones and teeth. Ironically, calcium's most important role is in bodily functions, such as muscle contraction and protein regulation. The body will

pull calcium from bones (causing problems like osteoporosis) if there is not enough of the element in a person's diet.

Phosphorus (1%) is found predominantly in bone but also in the molecule ATP, which provides energy in cells for driving chemical reactions.

Potassium (0.25%) is an important electrolyte (meaning it carries a charge in solution). It helps regulate the heartbeat and is vital for electrical signaling in nerves.

Sulfur (0.25%) is found in two amino acids that are important for giving proteins their shape.

Sodium (0.15%) is another electrolyte that is vital for electrical signalling in nerves. It also regulates the amount of water in the body.

Chlorine (0.15%) is usually found in the body as a negative ion, called chloride. This electrolyte is important for maintaining a normal balance of fluids.

Magnesium (0.05%) plays an important role in the structure of the skeleton and muscles. It is also necessary for more than 300 essential metabolic reactions.

Iron (0.006%) is a key element in the metabolism of almost all living organisms. It is also found in hemoglobin, which is the oxygen carrier in red blood cells. Half of all women do not get enough iron in their diet.

Fluorine (0.0037%) is found in teeth and bones. Outside of preventing tooth decay, it does not appear to have any importance to bodily health.

Zinc (0.0032%) is an essential trace element for all forms of life. Several proteins contain structures called 'zinc fingers' which help regulate genes. Zinc deficiency has been known to lead to dwarfism in developing countries.

Copper (0.0001%) is important as an electron donor in various biological reactions. Without enough copper, iron will not work properly in the body.

Iodine (0.000016%) is required for the making of thyroid hormones, which regulate metabolic rate and other cellular functions. Iodine deficiency, which can lead to goiter and brain damage, is an important health problem throughout much of the world.

Selenium (0.000019%) is essential for certain enzymes, including several antioxidants. Unlike animals, plants do not appear to require selenium for survival, but they do absorb it, so there are several cases of selenium poisoning from eating plants grown in selenium-rich soils.

Chromium (0.0000024%) helps regulate sugar levels by interacting with insulin, but the exact mechanism is still not completely understood.

Manganese (0.000017%) is essential for certain enzymes, in particular those that protect mitochondria – the place where usable energy is generated inside cells – from dangerous oxidants.

Molybdenum (0.000013%) is essential to virtually all life forms. In humans, it is important for transforming sulfur into a usable form. In nitrogen-fixing bacteria, it is important for transforming nitrogen into a usable form.

Cobalt (0.0000021%) is contained in vitamin B12, which is important in protein formation and DNA regulation.

As further research is done into the decline in global human health, I believe the fundamental importance that trace minerals play will become far more appreciated. They are a vital requirement for being genuinely healthy. The very best way you and your family can make sure you are achieving peak physical and mental health is by eating an organically homegrown plant-based diet[127] containing all these wonderful elements. We already have a vast amount of research to support the claims, but more and more will be produced over the coming years.

Those who are wise and create their Smart Garden today will benefit from far better physical and mental health for themselves and their family. They will be reaping the rewards long before a home food garden is either a mandated government requirement (as in Cuba) or becomes a status symbol for health and security.

Everyone will recognise that having a bountiful organic Smart Garden in your home guarantees you are harvesting the health-giving goodness from it. You will not only be enjoying better health but all the other benefits we will dive into now.

MATTER OF TASTE

'I have the simplest tastes. I am always satisfied with the best.'

– Oscar Wilde, poet and playwright

No one can deny that when you pick a fresh vegetable, it tastes infinitely better than something you could purchase from a store. 'It just tastes healthier', or 'It has more flavour', or 'It tastes sweeter' are common phrases used to describe the difference. That perceived increase in healthiness and flavour is our bodies' finely tuned, innate knowledge about what they need to be their most healthy. It is our biological conditioning from thousands of years of eating this way. When we eat something fresh, our bodies know that it has the vitamins, elements, macro and micronutrients, enzymes and natural sugars that signify a superior source.[128]

Our bodies are designed to assess what we consume in the very first instance that we place an item in our mouths. It tells us in subtle ways that this is good for us and we should find more. It also prompts us to store the knowledge of what it looked like and where we found it. It is probably one of the best examples of how innately we are connected to the earth and the bounty it produces.

Our body also tells us when we eat something we should not have. In cases like poisoning, it will make us faint, so we are forced to lie down and hopefully rest our way through the poisoning. Again, we store knowledge of what not to eat in future.

One of the concerning issues with the way our bodies innately understand food is that much of what we eat today is treated by our bodies as part toxin. This is caused by pollution,[129] contamination,[130] chemical additives,[131] high-temperature cooking[132] or processing.[133] When we consume a sugar-laden mega cup of soft drink from a fast-food store, our body goes into toxic shock. It attempts to fight the toxins created by the sugar content. While that is happening, our bodies have reduced immunity to bacterias and viruses. One of the ways our bodies respond to toxic food is to reduce our energy levels drastically. By making us lethargic, our bodies can conserve enough energy to fight the toxic food we have consumed. This might go some way to explaining the declining energy levels of our populations and the rise in sedentary-related disease like obesity.[134,135]

There is also a mental wellness benefit from the taste of your own homegrown food.

Knowing that what you are eating was planted and tended lovingly by you creates an incredible sense of wellbeing and empowerment. To use a well-known quote, 'Nothing tastes sweeter than the taste of success.' When you have travelled the life journey of a tiny seed to a harvested vegetable, it is one of the simplest but greatest joys we can experience. It profoundly speaks to the deepest parts of our humanity.

REDUCE YOUR IMPACT

'Nobody made a greater mistake than he who did nothing because he could do only a little.'

– Unknown

Today, many of us are at least aware of the fact we are dramatically harming the Earth. Many of the behaviours that make up our repeated daily habits and routines are responsible for the most damage. Some of us are trying to change those habits and patterns and are actively implementing alternatives. A Smart Garden can not only serve our needs but also help heal our fragile global environment.

Suppose we review the environmental impact created from the food we buy in a traditional supermarket. In that case, we can quickly see that any reduction in the amount we purchase will lessen that impact in a genuinely meaningful way.

Information from the Australian Bureau of Statistics shows that in 2015–16 the average Australian household spent $236.97 a week on food and non-alcoholic beverages. Interestingly, the mean amount of household income spent on vegetables across low- to high-income countries is only 4.74 per cent.[136] Data from the Australian Bureau of Agricultural and Resource Economics and Sciences show that in 2015–16, fruit and vegetables accounted for only 12.7 per cent of the total household food spend. Total food spend accounted for 16.2 per cent of the mean after-tax household income. To clarify, a household with a pre-tax income of $83,824 spent $11,826 on food per year. Only $1501.90 was spent on fruit and vegetables, which is the equivalent of $28.88 per week for the entire household.[137]

We are bombarded with government and community service marketing campaigns promoting the importance of fresh food for good health. So while fresh food is presented as the best way to achieve maximal health, it is easy to see that fresh produce represents only a tiny part of a weekly food consumption pattern. I am sure similar percentages for the weekly spend on fresh produce would be the same in other developed Western countries.

With only $11.41 being spent per person per household on fruit and vegetables, representing less than 12.7 per cent of our total food spend, we need to radically increase the amount of fresh produce we consume if we are to become a healthy community.[138]

It makes far more sense from both a health and environmental perspective to make this much-needed increase in fresh vegetable and produce consumption by growing it yourself. Your organic Smart Garden will not be adding to the plastic pollution of the Earth or increasing the use of chemical pesticides or herbicides. It will also not support climate change or soil erosion or add thousands of carbon miles to your dinner plate.

Research has shown that individual plastic use in the US amounts to just over 105 kilograms per person per year. If we are only effectively recycling 9 per cent of that plastic as research shows (even if we have adopted a 100 per cent efficient plastic-recycling program at home), it would mean that over 90 kilograms of the plastic we are recycling will still end up as some form of pollution, either via incineration or as landfill.[139]

Fresh produce, as it is currently sold in many supermarkets, requires excessive usage of single-use plastics. By increasing the purchase of our fresh produce at supermarkets, we will also be further adding to our personal pollution footprint. A Smart Garden is the perfect way to add organic, nutrient-dense health-giving fresh produce to your family's diets while reducing this footprint.

It only takes some simple maths to realise that the more your fresh produce needs are supplied by your home garden, the more you will reduce your plastic usage. A relatively small change towards self-sufficiency would create marked reductions in your plastic use. Let's say you currently recycle 10 kilograms of plastic, which goes into today's inefficient recycling programs. You would quickly and greatly reduce the amount of plastic packaging you bring home from the supermarket if you were growing some of your own produce. More importantly, home gardens reduce the net use of plastics altogether by not creating the need in the first place.

Another environmental benefit your Smart Garden offers is reducing the use and reliance on pesticides and herbicides. Not only will you and your family be enjoying produce that is free of chemical residues, and avoiding the myriad health and disease-related concerns that surround inadvertent chemical consumption, you will also be effectively using your hip pocket (spending power) to help drive change.

A small home Smart Garden growing a range of fresh produce is, by its diversity, less prone to infestation from insects and pests than large acres of mono-crops. Healthy, biologically enriched soil also creates far better plant health as it acts as a natural pesticide. The exact mechanisms of how healthy plants ward off insects and disease are still being researched, but some theories include:

1. Healthy plants give off infrared radiation and specific vibrations that are different from unhealthy plants. Insects, in particular, are attuned to this and will attack a sick plant first.[140]
2. Healthy plants can produce certain compounds that equate to natural pesticides and repel insects through a combination of smell and taste.[141]
3. Healthy plants are too nutrient enriched for insects to consume due to their simple (by human comparison) digestive systems.[142]

Whatever the exact mechanism, healthy soil and, in turn, healthy plants lead to far fewer pest and insect infestations. Your Smart Garden will supply you with a fresh bounty of produce without the requirement of any synthetic chemicals needed to control pests and insects. Not only will you be able to lessen your contribution to the growing global use of agrochemicals, but you will also no longer be inadvertently consuming trace amounts of the chemicals in the food you eat.

The same will hold true for the whole range of chemical-based herbicides that are used in industrial agriculture. While herbicides have many different ways of killing plants, they fall into two main categories: selective and non-selective. As the chemical companies' marketing information will tell you, a selective herbicide will only affect a targeted plant type or species.

This research is predominantly related to crop production. It refers to the herbicide's ability to kill the weeds present in the cropping area selectively. What is not researched is what other plant types could also be affected downstream of the application area. When a 'selective' herbicide enters a waterway, non-targeted indigenous plant life could also be killed.

Non-selective herbicides will generally kill all plant life that they come into contact with and are much more damaging to the environment. Though different herbicides use several additional mechanisms to inhibit growth and plant cell functions, they are all toxic to animals and humans. Other than their evident impact on the environment, they also promote pestilence. They make plants unhealthy, attracting more insects to feed on the ailing plants. These infestations often require the further use of pesticides to manage the insects.

Many weeds are becoming resistant to herbicides. This requires farmers to use higher and higher dosages to achieve previous results. This increase has meant that actual crops have had to be genetically engineered to be impervious to the herbicides and the contamination levels present in the soil.

These genetically modified crop types, be it corn, soy or wheat, have been bred with very little research on how this genetic modification may have impacted the plant's ability to absorb beneficial nutrients and minerals from the soil. Anti-herbicide lobby groups also claim that eating these genetically modified crops affects our body's ability to absorb nutrients and minerals.

I find another aspect of genetically modified herbicide-resistant crops even more concerning when we focus on our future global food security. The genetic modification of crops and plants has allowed the chemical companies that have funded the research to create new and novel crop breeds, to which they then register a legal patent. This has meant that chemical companies have been able to use the licensing of seeds to force farmers to use specific seed varieties and the chemical programs created for them.[143]

Suppose the farmer wishes to use a different, non-genetically modified seed or use organic growing methods in an area where the GM seeds are widely used. In that case, they open themselves to legal issues. If the registered GM plants grow in their paddocks, they can then be sued by the chemical companies.

Often wind drift can cause such seed movement between neighbouring farms. Farmers have seen their livelihoods destroyed by corporate lawyers who claim the farmer has 'stolen' a GM seed type without signing the necessary agreements and paying the companies for their use.[144] As it currently stands in industrial agriculture, these chemical companies effectively own and control every aspect of growing and production. The farmer has little opportunity to move away from the farming practice status quo, even if he wanted to adopt more sustainable methods.

Your organic Smart Garden will give you peace of mind knowing you are no longer supporting this system: a system that is poisoning our children's future natural capital and allowing further corporatisation of the agricultural industry.

Farmers are ultimately driven by consumer demand. They need to grow the crops and food that consumers want to purchase for themselves and their families. Generally speaking, they are incredibly responsive to market changes. They need to be for their survival. Suppose consumer demand shows they need to grow more nutritious crops using sustainable methods that help rebuild environments. In that case, that is what they will do.

By creating your Smart Garden, you will be benchmarking the changes consumers now require from their food. The produce from your organic home garden will be a new standard which commercial producers will need to replicate on a larger scale. You will be helping to change the future of consumer food demand. By sharing your Smart Garden produce with your neighbours, they too will find it hard to accept the produce they find at the local supermarket.

Consider the rise of the gourmet food industry over the last 20 years. People are highly motivated to feel they are consuming something that has been grown or created in an ideal or specialised way. It is extremely challenging for any of us to accept inferior products when we know others enjoy the superior products' benefits.

Suppose you are concerned with the direction of the current industrialised food system and all the impacts it is having on destroying the global environment. In that case, a Smart Garden offers you a perfect way to make a difference. As a by-product of eating great-tasting, healthy food, you will also be dramatically decreasing your personal impact on the environment by reducing your reliance on plastics, synthetic chemicals and petrochemicals while also lessening your contribution to soil erosion and greenhouse gas emissions.

A Smart Garden is one cost-effective and easy way for you to make a meaningful difference.

REAL FOOD SECURITY

'The average person is still under the aberrant delusion that food should be somebody else's responsibility until I'm ready to eat it.'

– Joel Salatin, author, lecturer, farmer and current owner of Polyface Farm in Swoope, Virginia

As part of your homegrown answer to the question of your future food security, your Smart Garden can offer you absolute peace of mind. It will provide you and your family with an insurance policy quite like no other. While we do not think twice about taking out insurance on homes, cars and personal belongings that we do not want stolen, lost or damaged, very few of us have any insurance against going hungry. This is a much bigger issue than having healthy food to eat. This issue affects one of our most basic requirements.

If you asked anybody what their basic needs were to ensure their survival, you would probably be offered an array of choices based on personal history, political leanings and general worldview. Our history shows there are just a couple of these needs that are genuinely universal.

The three needs that will have to appear based on our most basic physical survival requirement will be shelter, water and food. While the order can change depending on how harsh the natural environment of where you live is, these represent our most basic needs. Without these needs being met, we will be facing death in reasonably short order. As it is the basis for this book, we will focus on the food aspect for the moment.

Our need for food is critical to our ability to stay alive. Studies on how long we can live without food vary depending on our individual health and biological makeup. Generally, it is thought that after suffering from 30 days of starvation, most of us would already be dead. Starvation is something that has happened throughout human history, and our bodies are built to withstand it. Our biological systems and metabolism change markedly in times of starvation in an attempt to give us the very best chance of survival.

Millions of people die of starvation every year. That number could rise dramatically with the realities of future pandemics, climate change and natural disasters. In developed countries, we have been made to feel somewhat immune to the threat of not having enough food to eat.

Worryingly, the American Bureau of Statistics posted a report showing that 30 million Americans had presented to various support agencies as not having enough food to eat in June 2020.[145] If this situation can happen in one of the world's wealthiest countries, and we are just beginning to feel the effects of the post-pandemic economic reality, we are all at some risk.

There is already uncertainty around the ability of our present industrialised food system to meet current, let alone future, challenges. The potential for us to become food insecure and face food shortages is not some arbitrary threat but has become much more real.

The impetus to start building your food insurance policy today is increasing. There could quickly come a time when your ability to purchase the items necessary to create your own Smart Garden could become challenging as well.

When the COVID-19 pandemic just started to emerge, my wife and I went to our local garden centre to purchase some extra seeds. We felt it was prudent to load our garden up with an additional round of winter plantings as insurance against the pandemic – the outcome of which was then very much unknown.

We both stood in front of the edible seed section in disbelief. Every single seed packet had already been sold, and the display rack stood empty. We felt we had been extremely proactive in trying to access some extra seeds for planting, only to find that we had already left it too late. When we asked the garden centre employee when the seeds would be restocked, she just shrugged her shoulders, shook her head and told us she did not know.

Scarcity creates an anxious, hollow feeling in those of us who have enjoyed a lifetime of unlimited supply and abundance. It makes us feel caught out. The reality that we may not be able to provide for the basic needs of our loved ones is something that none of us can initially process. While the vast majority of people around the world face shortages of essential items like this every day, those of us who enjoy the privilege of living in developed economies have become dangerously complacent.

I once had to deliver firewood to a very elderly gentleman who lived in a suburb not far from our farm. After I finished unpacking the load for him, he kindly invited me in for a cup of tea. As I walked through his house to the kitchen, I could not help but notice large bags of flour, stores of canned food and other essential food items stocked through his home. I could not resist asking him why he had this apparent surplus of food stock. He told me he had lived through the Second World War as a young child in Europe and that you needed to have experienced that kind of thing only once to make sure that you always had some insurance against it happening again.

We have become so incredibly complacent in our belief that the system we rely on to feed ourselves is impervious to anything the future may have in store for us. We have lived through one of the most extended periods of peace and prosperity the world has ever seen, so why wouldn't we believe that to be true? It is that complacency that places us most at risk.

On average, people living in developed economies spend several thousand dollars annually on insurance. Yet, you have only a 1.9 per cent chance of having your home robbed, and you will have a collision in your car only once every 17.9 years. There is only a 0.125 per cent chance your house will burn down in the next 12 months. Despite all the relatively modest odds of something occurring to our possessions, we are still compelled to have some form of insurance that can offer us protection against adverse events.

Wouldn't it be equally justified to have some form of insurance around one of your three most basic needs for survival?

For the last 50 years, we have not perceived any real risk to us quickly dropping into the local supermarket to purchase all the things we believe we need. Of course, we are coerced by various means to purchase large amounts of things we do not need. The supply shortages we have all seen with the COVID-19 pandemic has been our first experience that the system can break down. Supermarket shelves can be empty, and resupply timelines unknown.

In assessing the suitability of any insurance policy, one of the most important aspects to consider is whether we will be able to access the benefits the policy offers when we need it most. Our newsfeeds often contain stories of individuals who, after experiencing a catastrophic event in their lives, attempt to access the well-planned insurance policy's benefits only to find the benefit is unavailable. This can be for various reasons, as many insurance companies have turned payout avoidance into an art form.

Access to the benefits of your insurance policy is critical to the appropriateness of the policy itself. Your Smart Garden can provide you with an insurance policy against not having access to food. The fact your garden will be within the confines of your property boundary ensures its effectiveness to deliver when you need it most. Not only will it be safely accessible, but you will also be able to tend to your Smart Garden securely.

In the realities of the COVID-19 pandemic, we have all faced the unprecedented concept of community lockdown. In Australia, our lockdown rules stipulated that only one person from a household could go to the supermarket to purchase groceries. Many countries have had similar laws ordained in their communities and have had to endure increases in social unrest. Sending a loved one out alone into a situation of social and civil unrest created by communities who feel scared and vulnerable is far from ideal.

We have even seen some elements within communities who take advantage of certain conditions and control an area in a town or city, such as in Seattle with the forming of CHAZ or the Capitol Hill Autonomous Zone in 2020. The very best option in these situations is for you and your family to remain together and at home.

In these circumstances, your Smart Garden becomes your super-safe supermarket at home. The ability to access fresh produce to feed your family during such events cannot be oversold. It is an insurance policy you know can and will deliver when you need it most.

Your Smart Garden will not only always be there for you, but the amount of food you can access will not be limited by government decree or law changes. We have seen buying limits imposed by food suppliers on essential items to restrict hoarding and surplus buying from the public.

In our situation with six children, any weekly grocery shop would easily look like hoarding, especially compared to an average couple's grocery shop. We also prefer, for economic reasons, to shop once every couple of months. We do this because of a reason I outlined earlier. We all fall prey to the situation where we go to the supermarket to buy a few simple items and somehow come home with many ancillary items! Somehow a quick trip to grab some milk becomes an exercise in blowing our weekly budget.

We do our grocery shopping only three or four times a year. We endure the strange looks and muted comments while standing at the checkout with five trolleys of non-perishable foodstuffs and household items. We have calculated that it saves us several thousand dollars per year, as we do not fall into the trap of the weekly 'oh, but I'll also just grab that while I'm here' extra costs. It also means should anything happen, we always have several weeks/months of essential items in storage at our home.

Before we changed our shopping habits, we found that no matter how hard we tried not to be swayed by the 'promotions' and 'specials' on offer, we often came home with more than we intended to buy. There is a psychological reason that the bread and milk are found at the back of the supermarket. You are forced to walk by an entire store's worth of products to get access to these essentials. We found that the only effective way to mitigate this and stick to our family budget was to stop going frequently to the supermarket. Our four-monthly shop is our way not to be suckered into feeding our consumer addictions.

Our preference for bulk shopping also had benefits during the lockdowns. The problem with strictly adhering to store-imposed buying limits of one or two items per customer is that it will never cover a large family's needs. Sending a single family member out every day or two, as mandated by the government, might not be advisable if they are at greater risk by leaving your home.

Your Smart Garden cannot, of course, supply you with fresh milk or bread (unless you are very creative!). Still, it can offer you a stop-gap when our society's regular operation might be impacted by circumstances or events like a pandemic or natural disaster.

CREATING GREEN MONEY

'All wealth comes from Nature. Without it, there wouldn't be any economics. The primary wealth is food, not money.'

– Margaret Atwood, *Payback: Debt and the Shadow Side of Wealth*

Your Smart Garden can also be an income source for you and your family in times of economic uncertainty and higher unemployment rates. It can provide you with not only a cash income but the ability to barter and trade. The things that hold or increase value when economic times become difficult are always essential commodities. Commodities are defined as 'a useful or valuable thing that can be traded', and there are not many things as useful or as valuable as fresh food.

It is not just in tough economic times that your Smart Garden provides this added income-producing ability. You will also be able to barter, trade, or help support and build your community with the tasty offerings from your Smart Garden in the good times as well. With the rise in popularity of the 'sharing economy' and the meteoric growth in internet-based businesses like Airbnb and Uber, the premise of collaborative consumption and peer-to-peer exchange will likely be a growth sector in the broader economy in the future.

The ability to connect to a marketplace of consumers could help overcome one of the main problems with traditional bartering or fresh produce trading. Bartering or trading has always relied on the two individual needs aligning so a trade could take place. If no one in your immediate location wanted your fresh broccoli, you would be unable to trade, particularly if you needed something specific in return, like bread, for example.

Historians have noted that while bartering and trade in commodities have taken place since the earliest times of humanity, it rarely existed as the sole basis of any economic activity. But when the prevailing financial system collapsed, bartering became the only way people could survive. A more widely used version of bartering has been far more prevalent and carries greater altruistic significance. What has always been an essential part of human culture, rooted in our survival mechanism, is better termed as 'gifting'. Gifting relied far less on the immediate need to find someone who needed your specific goods or services. It has underpinned the transactional premise for communities whose collective welfare was considered critical to the individuals' survival.

Gifting is where you would offer your goods or services to someone else with the knowledge that they would provide you with something in return of equal value at a later date. This gifting process would be the foundation of holistic cooperative communities. Everyone was motivated to play an active role within it for their own and the community's survival. It would be relatively easy to see if anyone were taking advantage of the situation for their own personal gain without returning in kind the things they had received. Everyone within the community could create value through either goods they had produced or the trade of services or labour. A gifting economy is driven by acknowledged responsibilities, first to you and your family and then to your extended family, friends, neighbours and ultimately to your wider community.

Our current Western economies are incredibly isolating to the individuals within them. Using currency conceived through debt creation essentially burdens people into a cycle of debt that lasts their lifetime. The ability to gift, barter or trade with a physical commodity like fresh produce from your garden allows you to participate actively in a caring community's proper functioning.

Your Smart Garden can provide you with real physical cash income by attending markets to sell your produce. These range from simple car boot markets to huge organic farmers' markets that can have hundreds of stallholders. These types of markets have exploded in popularity in recent years for several reasons. One of the primary drivers is that it helps connect people with their food producers and gives them a unique insight into the methods and philosophy of the grower.

Gemma and I have had stalls at markets like this for many years, selling a variety of different produce. We have managed to meet fantastic like-minded people and share in the market 'community' while earning an income from our stall. By far, the busiest stalls at markets such as these are the ones that are selling fresh produce. While there is a fair amount of work involved in the preparation, set-up and sale of your produce, you will be almost certainly assured of selling your produce to the many happy buyers in attendance.

Before the beginning of the industrial revolution, this type of 'self-employment' was how much of the population would make a living.[146] The predominance of agrarian communities skews this, but it is also a fact that we have been living and thriving by this method of working and earning a living for far longer than we have been a slave to a wage.

There is something truly empowering about growing or making something and then receiving payment for it from a delighted customer. It places you in direct control and responsible for your own destiny. Your labour truly becomes your reward. As with any act of human endeavour, you will have good days and bad days, but these will be *your* good days and bad days. The tiredness you feel at the end of the market will be your tiredness. You will have the inner peace of knowing that the Smart Garden you had the vision to create and nurture is returning to you in kind.

Another way your Smart Garden will offer you economic benefits is as a hedge against deflation and inflation. The consensus between economic commentators in recent times is that we are likely to see a period of deflation and then inflation over the next decade.

Deflation will affect consumer prices by seeing them further reduced. While on the surface this would sound like a good thing, much of what we purchase, particularly fresh produce, is already priced at a level that makes it difficult for farmers to produce. Further deflation could easily make the production of certain produce economically unviable.

For every single $1 of produce sold at retail prices in a supermarket, the farmer is only receiving on average 7.8 cents in revenue.[147] The other 92.2 cents comprises all the additional production costs, taxes and profit margins after the produce has left the farmer's gate. Suppose farmers can no longer afford to survive in a deflationary economic environment. In that case, we will see it reflected in empty shelves at our supermarkets.

Your Smart Garden will be there to make up these shortfalls in production and ensure you can supplement your fresh food supply should things we currently take for granted become unavailable.

If, as is currently being forecast, we then enter into a period of inflation in the next decade, we will see prices rise, possibly exponentially from what we enjoy today. Not only does an inflationary economic environment cause prices to rise, but it may also impact expenditures like mortgage repayment costs, because central banks generally raise interest rates in response to inflation to try to slow it down. Inflation becomes a double bind of higher consumer prices and less disposable income.

By having a Smart Garden, you will be producing a raw commodity – food – that will be benefiting from this inflationary environment. The value of all your produce will be increasing, and not only will that buffer you against the rising supermarket costs of the same item, but it will also help reduce your expenditure because you do not have to purchase that item.

I like to think of a Smart Garden as a 'green bank'. The things you produce in your garden need to be seen as 'money in the bank'. Your 'green bank' will not only genuinely save you money, but it can provide you with actual money or the means from which you can barter, trade or even gift to others in need. It will act as a hedge against uncertain times. If conditions worsen, it will add further value to your garden. It becomes the very definition of an asset. Your garden will be what accountants refer to as a tangible asset, as it is a physical thing that can increase in value.

I believe we will see far greater capital investment into actual farmland and agricultural commodities in the future. On a macro level, that is where the laws of supply and demand and scarcity will offer future investors their most significant returns. Your Smart

Garden will be your micro-investment into the very same market; large investors like Bill Gates are seeing these commodities as one of the best future opportunities. Their investment, though, will simply be financial numbers on a computer screen. If computer screens go blank for any reason, they will not have just lost access to their money but to the tangible assets as well.

Unlike these investors, you will be able to see, smell and taste your tangible asset and investment by merely going to your back door and taking a few steps to your Smart Garden.

Another financial aspect to consider is if we measure the nutritional benefits of eating from our own Smart Garden versus eating store-bought produce. We can easily see the cost savings that a garden can provide for you. You can produce a weekly garden bounty for about the same amount as the savings on your weekly grocery bill, depending on how much fresh produce you would typically buy. If, on average, your home garden produces food that is two to three times more nutritious than a similar store-bought variety, then you are receiving much more value than the store-bought items offer.

As supermarket food prices increase, as I believe they will do over the next decade, your garden will allow you to save more of your hard-earned money and provide even more value!

FUNCTIONAL FOOD

'Functional foods are foods that have a potentially positive effect on health beyond basic nutrition. Proponents of functional foods say they promote optimal health and help reduce the risk of disease.'

– Katherine Zeratsky, registered dietitian nutritionist at the Mayo Clinic

Your Smart Garden can also act as a preventative medicine source for you and your family. As we have covered earlier in this book, and as championed by health officials the world over, nothing beats a healthy diet for promoting and sustaining long-term human health.

In the 1980s, Japan was the first to coin the term 'functional food' as part of a diet-led health drive by medical officials and the government.[148] Foods were given this title if it was believed their nutritional profiles also meant they offered consumers other benefits, like reducing the prevalence of disease and ill health. Medical research has shown that many conditions result from insufficiency or over-supply of certain nutrients, minerals and compounds. This has led to the promotion of the concept of a 'balanced diet' and 'recommended daily allowances' of vitamins and minerals.

So, another benefit of your Smart Garden will be its ability to reduce your family's medical costs. Medical costs can be a considerable burden on a family's budget. Chronic disease and illness can easily bankrupt families who were once financially secure. This financial burden is increased in countries that do not have a social healthcare system. In the US, for example, the average American spends $5000 per person on medical-related expenses per year.[149] It also has one of the unhealthiest populations with increasing rates of diet-related diseases like obesity and diabetes. As a consequence of eating from your garden and achieving better health, you will be financially better off by reducing your chances of suffering from preventable disease and illness.

While researching what is driving our increasing healthcare costs, it was revealed that 'unhealthy behaviours and diets' are considered the most significant single issue.[150]

It struck me as extraordinarily peculiar that as 'unhealthy behaviours and diets' are the primary driver of rising healthcare costs,[151] improving and increasing 'healthy behaviours and diets' is not more widely promoted as a solution.

Could it be that 'unhealthy behaviours and diets' are a critical economic driver in our modern society? Could any meaningful positive change to these 'unhealthy behaviours and diets' hurt corporate bottom lines? This might well explain why being 'healthier' is often placed at the bottom of the list of ways to reduce health costs.

The global food industry makes billions of dollars every year by harming our populations by taking advantage of their 'unhealthy behaviours and diets'. The medical sector then gets to make billions of dollars every year, keeping people productive and merely alive.

There is a substantial economic incentive to not change the status quo. Large food corporations are the real gatekeepers of this cycle. Their powerful food and beverage lobby groups hide in the shadows of our public health systems' political processes.

A Smart Garden is your chance to remove yourself from this cycle of iniquity. Not only does your garden help remove your need to buy into these 'unhealthy behaviours and diets', but it will improve your health and reduce your potential for disease. In turn, these factors reduce your need to buy into the medical mouse wheel set up to fix them. By taking a more active role in and responsibility for your health with the simple act of actively growing some, if not all, of your fresh produce requirements, you can save real money at both ends of this spectrum.

When you cost out your Smart Garden's creation, it is essential to factor in all the potential savings and benefits that come with its realisation. Reducing your medical costs is just one of the many benefits your garden offers you and your family. It is perhaps also the one benefit that is impossible to truly calculate if it plays a role in your family never developing a preventable disease or ill-health. The real question is, perhaps, what would you be willing to pay to reduce the likelihood of yourself or a loved one dying a diet-related premature death?

There are many nutritious plants that you can grow in your home garden that have been proven to have either high levels of specific vitamins and minerals when compared to other plants or offer a more extensive array of vitamins and minerals.

Kale is often promoted as the king of the leafy green varieties because it offers an abundance of vitamins, including vitamins C, A, K1 and B6, and minerals such as magnesium, calcium, copper and manganese.

Magnesium plays an essential role in keeping us fit. Though we still do not fully understand all of the intricate biological interactions between our bodily systems and magnesium, we know that deficiencies can cause a host of adverse health consequences. Research for the US National Institutes of Health found:

> Magnesium deficiency can cause a wide variety of features including hypocalcemia, hypokalemia and cardiac and neurological manifestations. Chronic low magnesium state has been associated with many chronic diseases including diabetes, hypertension, coronary heart disease, and osteoporosis.[152]

While magnesium can be found in various foodstuffs, it is highly bioavailable in the leafy greens that can be quickly grown in a Smart Garden. Plants like kale, spinach and Asian greens can ensure you and your family can access many of the vitamins and minerals needed to build and maintain good health.

In a situation where pharmaceutical medicines became more challenging to access, knowing that your garden supplies you with the recommended daily allowances of these critical vitamins and minerals would offer real peace of mind. Knowing you are not only able to maintain good health but actively reduce your risk of disease and illness makes a great preventative health strategy. It reinforces the widespread belief that an ounce of prevention is equal to a pound of cure.

While I have used magnesium as an example above for the potential disease risk from dietary deficiencies, other micronutrient deficiencies can also increase disease prevalence.

Your Smart Garden will also be a terrific source of vitamin C, vitamin A, iron, calcium and manganese, and many other essential vitamins and minerals. It is easy to see how your family's health will be the real winner. Many people already take specific vitamin supplements or multivitamin supplements in an attempt to achieve better health. Your garden will be your multivitamin and mineral source, and all the vitamins and minerals will be able to be processed by your body much more efficiently. The vegetables and produce you eat will also contain the specific enzymes needed to make them bioavailable to your body.

HEALTH AND LIFESTYLE BENEFITS

'One of the most important resources that a garden makes available for use, is the gardener's own body. A garden gives the body the dignity of working in its own support. It is a way of rejoining the human race.'

– Wendell Berry

STAYING ACTIVE

A garden provides you with real motivation to get up and about. An hour or two in your Smart Garden can offer you a gentle but effective workout. As we bend, lift and stretch doing our garden round of upkeep and harvesting, we are active. The major muscle groups we are using are the ones we need to keep more mobile, and we are building strength in areas of importance like our arms, legs and core. A Kansas State University study showed that getting older people to mix soil and fill pots to plant seeds improved hand strength and grip.[153]

Being active provides an essential aspect of being healthy, and your Smart Garden is a great gym alternative. Spending time in a garden is a good physical workout with the added benefit that it is not repetitive and doesn't have high injury incidence. The fact that you do not have to leave your home is another advantage, and you will not be using fossil fuel to get to your workout location.

KEEP THE WEIGHT OFF

Studies have shown that gardeners have lower body mass indexes (BMIs) than non-gardeners. One hour of diligent garden work can burn the equivalent of a gym session, or more than 300 calories.[154] Having a high BMI can lead to a whole host of problems like diabetes, high blood pressure and heart disease. An hour a day in the garden will work wonders for keeping the weight off.

REDUCE HEART DISEASE

A 12-year study in Sweden that involved 4000 adults showed that a physical activity like gardening could reduce the incidence of strokes and heart attacks by up to 30 per cent.[155] Again, it is about being active. The Department of Health in the UK has studies that show that a 10 per cent increase in average physical activity by adults would postpone 6000 deaths a year and save over £500 million annually.[156]

HELP FIGHT DEPRESSION

Spending time tending a garden is known to help enhance a sense of wellbeing and self-esteem, improve serotonin levels and reduce anxiety. Healthy, organic soil contains a beneficial bacterium known as *Mycobacterium vaccae* that directly lifts serotonin levels when we inhale it.[157]

If you have ever been in an abundant healthy garden, raised a handful of fresh soil to your nose and inhaled deeply, you will understand the feeling it immediately engenders. It is hard, if not impossible, to spend an hour in your garden and not come away with a lift to your mood and levels of happiness.

BRAIN FUNCTION AND AGEING

Issues with our brain health, particularly cognitive decline in our ageing population, is a growing trend. Forecasts show that by the year 2050, the current numbers of individuals over the age of 65 will double.[158] Cognitive decline in the elderly will increase social and medical costs to future generations as sufferers require additional care. Studies are now researching cognitive decline and impairment as a possible precursor to dementia.

A recent report in the *Journal of Neurology* highlighted research from Rush University in Chicago and the Tufts Human Nutrition Research Center on Aging in Boston. Their study showed that consuming one serve of leafy greens per day slowed cognitive decline in the elderly:

> In the study, consumption of green leafy vegetables was positively and significantly associated with slower cognitive decline. When comparing the highest daily consumption (median 1.3 servings a day) with the lowest (median 0.09 servings a day), the rate of cognitive decline among those who consumed the most to those who consumed the least was equivalent to being 11 years younger cognitively, based on average global cognitive scores over time. There was no evidence that the association was affected by cardiovascular conditions, depressive symptoms, low weight, or obesity.[159]

A Smart Garden is the best way to source these types of super-nutritious leafy green vegetables. You will be able to grow them organically and in biologically rich, living soils, and they are extremely good at taking care of themselves. Many of the leafy green varieties are among the easiest of all vegetables to grow and the most efficient and prolific at giving you large amounts of produce. They quickly provide the basis for fantastic plant-based diets and nutrition plans.

As we get older, making sure that our cognitive abilities remain their sharpest should be a priority for all of us. Knowing the difference just one serving of leafy green vegetables can make should further incentivise you to start your Smart Garden today.

SUPPORT THE CHANGE TO PLANT-BASED DIETS

The future of human diets is plant-based. No system is as harmful, wasteful or as patently iniquitous as industrial livestock farming. With so much of the human-edible crops we currently grow being fed to animals as livestock feed, and increasing global starvation rates, governments and agencies will have to redirect these supplies to starving human beings fighting for life.

Prioritising the production of premium cuts of meat for a wealthy fraction of the population over starving peoples is utterly unacceptable in a compassionate world. It takes on average 25 kilograms of feedstock to produce 1 kilogram of beef meat protein.[160] The livestock industry is the most resource-intensive, creates the most significant amount of environmental damage and is the cause of the highest level of adverse health outcomes of all food categories.

Your home Smart Garden will put you at the leading edge of this change to a plant-based diet and all the health and environmental benefits that come with it.

EXTEND YOUR LIFESPAN

Countries and regions that have been shown to have long-lived populations are often called Blue Zones by scientists. These Blue Zones are being researched to determine why some of us can live active, productive and relatively disease-free lives into our hundreds. This research has found a few commonalities in the people and communities that have active full lives to incredibly old ages.[161]

One of them is that these populations mostly have an agrarian-based existence. They are highly engaged in the production of their own food supply. Another is that the food they consume is predominantly plant-based.

The findings show that there are numerous physical health benefits to this type of lifestyle and diet. The mental and emotional benefits also play a significant role. People who feel that they have a deeper sense of purpose and the support of close communities have far lower stress levels and anxiety than typical Western populations. These benefits are an intrinsic part of agrarian-based communities. It is not hard to see why happier, healthier and less stressed people would live longer.

BUILD COMMUNITY

My grandfather talks about when his family, and almost all the people in his small coastal community, would grow much of their own food and supplement their diets with hunting and fishing. He describes how any oversupply to their needs would be 'passed over the fence' to a grateful neighbour. He talks fondly about how these small actions broke down barriers, created relationships and built close-knit communities.

The response that people have when you offer to share with them something you have grown in your garden is always one of delight and appreciation. You can derive much pride in knowing that you have proactively helped someone make ends meet and provided for them an extra boost of tasty produce and nutrition. It is a perfect icebreaker and conversation starter. We live in a world where neighbourly interactions have, in many cases, been reduced to quick smiles to each other as we fleetingly pass, leaving or entering our homes. It is hard to think of a better way to start rebuilding those connections than with the offer of a bunch of bright orange carrots or freshly picked basil.

PART THREE

YOUR SMART GARDEN: A 12-STEP PLAN

OUR (CONTINUING) ADVENTURE

'The most noteworthy thing about gardeners is that they are always optimistic, always enterprising, and never satisfied. They always look forward to doing something better than they have ever done before.'

– Vita Sackville-West, novelist, poet, journalist and avid gardener

I want to provide you with an overview of the things we have implemented in our garden that have massively reduced our workload and increased our yields. In the following chapters, we will look at the fantastic scientific and technological advancements that are happening in the world of home gardening.

Technically, what we have created on our farm to grow our family's food supply is a small-scale protected cropping environment. One of the fastest-growing areas in agriculture is protected cropping, and for incredibly good reasons. Protected cropping is defined as 'the production of fruits and vegetables within, under or sheltered by artificial structures and/or materials to provide and/or enable modified growing conditions and/or protection from pests and adverse weather'.[162]

Protected cropping incorporates the best aspects of many other growing methods, including greenhouse horticulture, plasticulture, low-cost protected cropping (LCPC) and controlled environment horticulture (CEH).

The exciting aspect of protected cropping as a methodology is that it benefits from a large amount of research and technological advancement. Individuals, farms and companies realise that while it can radically increase yields and reduce workloads, it also diminishes adverse climate effects and reduces the environmental impact of typical food production.

In the following chapters, we will look at how you can turn a traditional veggie garden concept into a food production system using the protected cropping methodologies. It was trial and error that led us to create this type of garden. It was only recently that we realised what we had built fell into a recognised horticultural category!

Our traditional outdoor garden needed a considerable amount of time and effort to manage. It was also at the mercy of the weather and pests. Our local possum population feasted on our crops over many years. Uncannily, this seemed to always happen just before harvest and after many weeks of effort and hard work. We tried everything from bird netting to salmon netting. While they all offered some protection, possums would often sit on the nets and still crush the struggling vegetables underneath them. Bird netting also has the disadvantage of stopping essential pollination from bees and other insects.

We tried various fencing types, including the humorously titled 'floppy fence' made with a floppy wire top piece that caused possums to feel unsafe climbing them. We also tried corrugated steel fences that were designed not to allow them grabbing points, and all the way to elaborate electric fences. While all the fence styles offered small amounts of extra protection, they all failed in some particular way to fully defend our precious garden beds. Not only did they ultimately prove ineffective, but there was also much work and cost in building fence style after fence style.

Another issue we had with the traditional outdoor garden model was the water supply. We always needed to use our household rain-water supply to water our gardens. Often in summer, this meant organising outside deliveries of water from our local water carriers. Not only is this expensive, but the water they bring you is typically town water and therefore treated with chemicals like chlorine and fluoride. After struggling for several years with various iterations of a traditional outdoor garden, we decided, in desperation, to build our first greenhouse.

A greenhouse is a great way to grow fruits and vegetables and they are used successfully worldwide. We have close friends with some of the largest greenhouses in Australia, and they use them to grow a range of flowers for florists across the country.

Building our greenhouse took about eight months and involved hundreds of hours of labour. As money was tight, Gemma and I did 90 per cent of the work ourselves, including hand-digging 32 holes, each 1.2 metres deep, in hard clay for our upright support poles. The building process required both Gemma and I to be scaling up and down ladders multiple times a day. As we neared completion of the greenhouse, I required minor surgery on both of my knees due to tears in the meniscus membrane from climbing the ladders repeatedly over many months.

It is worth every cent and hour (though I wouldn't recommend injury). The greenhouse is 200 square metres (2152 square feet) in size, or 10 metres wide by 20 metres long. It is built with outdoor timbers and clad in corrugated clear plastic panels. We created 75 square metres (807 square feet) of actual garden bed space in this area using a handmade raised bed design.

We decided to incorporate *Hügelkultur* in the filling of our garden beds. *Hügelkultur* is German for 'small hill' and was first developed by farmers in northern Europe. They created piles of semi-decaying wood and covered them with soil to make a garden bed mound. The benefits of this method are several-fold. The decaying wood generates heat which in turn warms the soil above. This improves the germination rate of any seeds planted into the ground. The wood also acts as a water sink. Excess rainfall is trapped in the wood as it acts like a sponge. This water is then drawn on by the soil and by the plants' root systems when water is in short supply. The wood also offers an ideal home for worms and microbes as it decays and will ultimately break down to a point where it just naturally becomes part of the soil profile.

With the expansive roof area of the greenhouse, we were now able to harvest rainfall for the garden and incorporate a solenoid-controlled dripline watering system. The roof area effectively doubled our rainwater harvesting ability. We direct this, very specifically, to the beds and plants that require watering.

Our watering system is run by a central control unit that allows us to set the amount of water flow and the specific day and time for it to occur. Healthy soil is made up in part by at least 30–40 per cent water content, so this is vital. Since the installation of the irrigation system, we have never had to worry about watering our garden. We only need to occasionally increase or decrease overall water flow to match ambient weather temperatures; that is, more water in summer and less in winter.

Part of our design for the greenhouse was to make it as accessible as we possibly could. We had learned over the years that the further away your garden is from your home, the less likely you are to attend to it. So it needed to be part of our daily lives as much as possible. We access our greenhouse from our main living area, so we walk from our lounge room area directly into our greenhouse. We designed the greenhouse to thermally heat our house for zero cost, a boon in reducing our overall power consumption.

We built our greenhouse to be a closed system. We intended to control the temperature within a few degrees, no matter what the outside temperature was at the time. We use temperature and humidity sensors (hygrometers) in key areas all around the greenhouse. These give us information about how hot and humid the greenhouse is on an LCD screen in our kitchen.

Unfortunately, we soon faced traditional greenhouse design issues, and new problems started to raise their ugly heads. Controlling an environment like a large greenhouse is incredibly energy-intensive. Our greenhouse is slightly larger than our home so, in effect, we now needed to heat and cool an area larger than our house. Though, unlike our home, with its fully insulated roof and walls, our greenhouse only had a thin sheet of transparent corrugated cladding to protect it from outside temperature variations.

To heat our garden in winter, we needed the largest non-commercial home gas heater we could buy. It proved to have almost no effect on raising the temperature in the greenhouse above the outside ambient temperatures, even when set to its highest output. We tried to make sure we had no areas that could be leaking heat, so we closed off all minor gaps and possible heat escape points. Then we started to notice that mould and mildew had begun appearing on the walls and some plants.

This required cleaning walls with mild bleaches and removing affected plants, which was not something we wanted to be doing in our organic garden! After in-depth discussions with several greenhouse experts, we believed we needed to install an array of fans to help circulate the air within the greenhouse and reduce the incidence of these moulds and mildews. This then reduced our heating system's effectiveness as the air movement lowered the greenhouse's ambient temperature.

Over the next few months, other issues emerged as the costs to control our greenhouse became too great. We decided we needed a new approach, and our Smart Garden concept first came to be.

We realised that our greenhouse quickly lost many of its 'sustainable' qualities as its energy requirements were outstripping any hard-won benefits. It also created several other issues, which all presented their unique challenges. One crucial problem we did not envisage was the disconnection the greenhouse created to our local gardening community. We had created a greenhouse garden environment that was very different from our geographical area, e.g. much hotter and more humid than a typical Tasmanian cool temperate climate. The plants and seeds from our local suppliers were not applicable to the environment within the greenhouse. We could not barter or trade our seeds and plants for theirs. Most of their gardens were outside and exposed to a completely different environment than the one created by our greenhouse.

We tried importing seeds from northern Australia, where it is hotter and more humid. That was not incredibly successful either.

Finally, we decided to make wholesale changes by opening up our greenhouse and removing several plastic panels from the walls and roof. We removed only a small panel area from the greenhouse side that was facing the prevailing wind direction. Our outdoor gardening experience has taught us that constant wind is a significant impediment to healthy high-yielding plants. Young seedlings devote much of their energy to growing additional root and stem material to fight against being blown down. This, in turn, reduces their ability to flourish and fruit.

We took several panels off the non-prevailing wind sides and replaced them with basic chicken wire mesh. Our local possum population's night-time raids were still thwarted, but now bees and other pollinating insects had access to our garden. By doing the same with a few strategically removed roof panels, we avoided creating the huge heat issues we battled in summer. The heated air would now expel through the vented roof system.

We then looked at the average rainfall pattern for our area. We set our irrigation system to replicate a 'good' year of rainfall. Our plants would now enjoy a life of consistent peak water access. Now we could also use locally attained and developed seeds and plant stock. They could enjoy all the very best of Tasmania's cool climate. At the same time, our protected garden environment sheltered them from the worst of the wind, rain, cold and heat. During our first harvest year with our new stripped-down greenhouse/protected Smart Garden, our yields doubled and, in some cases, tripled! We quickly realised that we were finally onto something.

Our new Smart Garden allows us to take the best outdoor and greenhouse aspects and combine them. This reduces or averts many of the problems and challenges that both methods have. The proof of concept is in the bounty of dark green edible vegetation that now proliferates in our garden. Friends and family enter our garden and slowly walk around, stunned at the abundance of fresh vegetables and fruit on offer. The living energy inside our garden seems to physically hum, as do the bees and insects that can come and go freely.

We are always trying new things and developing ideas and concepts. We have recently been doing much more with our soil health, compost and organic amendments with excellent results. This has allowed us to 'feed' off plants by taking small amounts from a plant without reducing its health or viability. Often in the past, when we would remove a few leaves from lettuce for a salad, we would see it slowly lose health and become more susceptible to insect infestation and disease. Now we can take a basket into our garden and harvest parts of plants for our meal with no negative impacts on the plant. For us, this is a by-product of having excellent soil health and making available to the plant all the nutrients and minerals it needs to be in the best health and condition.

We are rebuilding and adding a range of composted manures and plant waste materials to our soils several times a year now. The results again speak for themselves.

Our Smart Garden is a passion project and, as such, a constant work in progress. We learn more and more with every moment we spend there, and for us, it is a place of innovation and research. We are continually trying new things and approaches to grow more nutrient-dense food and reduce the time and effort needed to create it. It is a place of intense education, not only for Gemma and myself but also for our children. The best part of such a learning environment is that all the lessons are valuable and essential. They represent the true definition of life lessons.

In the following chapters, we will overview many of the things you should consider when planning and creating your own Smart Garden. It is by no means exhaustive as your garden requirements will be governed by many factors, including your needs, expectations, location and lifestyle. There are thousands of great books on the 'how to's' of planting and growing vegetables and fruits. Part of your Smart Garden journey is finding the information that specifically applies to you and what you want to eat and achieve.

Your Smart Garden and the technograrian food production method are umbrella concepts on how you can maximise the production and benefits, and minimise your garden's time requirement, cost and effort. Let us look at some of the factors that you will need to consider and more of the concepts and ideas that are part of the decision-making process.

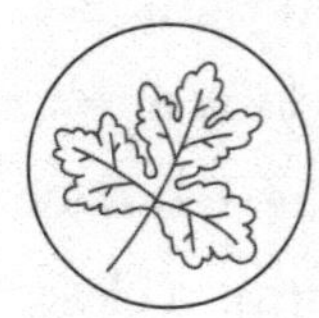

CREATING YOUR SMART GARDEN

'To plant a garden is to believe in tomorrow.'

– Audrey Hepburn, actress and humanitarian

The things we like to eat can be particular and limited. Still, a Smart Garden is a great way to expand your diet to include a much more extensive range of healthy fresh produce.

A diet that is predominantly plant-based allows you to supply more of your personal needs from your garden. You will need to look at long-term storage solutions for your harvests to maximise your garden's ability to feed you year-round. As with any of the 'old arts' that we incorporate into our farm lifestyle, they can initially seem overwhelmingly complicated and time-consuming. As with any acquired skill, though, the practice quickly improves outcomes and in the time it used to take us to bottle 12 jars of pasta sauce, we can now do 120!

For us, our garden readily supplies 70–80 per cent of the food we eat in any given week. Our diets are predominantly vegetarian.

We can grow a range of vegetables and fruits in our garden and use bottling, pickling, dehydration and freezing techniques to make sure nothing is ever wasted and our produce is available year-round. Any green waste is composted or fed to animals like our chickens that then, in order, produce eggs.

We suggest you always frame your objective in all your garden activities to create closed, sustainable loops. Green waste, chickens and eggs is perhaps the perfect example of a closed sustainable loop. The green waste (parts of a plant we have grown but don't eat) are fed to our chickens, who produce protein-rich eggs that we then consume to give us the energy to work in our garden. We also use nitrogen-abundant chicken manure to fertilise our garden. Everyone is happy, and there is no waste. This fantastic closed sustainability loop can happen in a small suburban backyard, and chickens make the best pets!

If you are trying to feed a family from your Smart Garden, you will need to also look at your fresh produce consumption levels in a typical week. One piece of advice is that you will need more space than you probably initially believe. Packing many plants and vegetables into a small area is a recipe for disease and low yields. There is a sweet spot for planting density that maximises your space and your yield. Speak to local gardeners or research on the internet to find spacing suggestions on the plant variety you are working with.

Look at what you are currently buying in your fresh produce shopping and see what you could feasibly grow in your garden. Your Smart Garden will allow you to grow not only a more extensive range of produce but will also extend the viable season for growing. This means you might be able to double harvest (plant two crop cycles) of slower growing plants and add another two or three cycles of faster-growing stagger-planted produce (new plantings made weekly of the same crop).

Many of the fresh produce items we purchase are incredibly easy to grow in our own Smart Garden. Spinach, lettuce, spring onions, beets, kale, Asian greens, cucumbers, tomatoes, zucchini, beans and so on are all shopping list staples. They can be quickly grown by even the most novice of Smart Gardeners.

When considering the food you would like to eat from your Smart Garden, consider your newfound ability to create a range of chutneys, pickles, jams and preserves. Every year we use the last of the chillies from our harvest to make the chilli jam for our winter menu and snacks. While we use a base recipe, we continuously experiment with added flavours and ingredients, so no two years are ever the same. It can generate considerable nostalgia when we remember back to the excellent chilli jam of 2014. Like a winemaker and the vineyard, we connect to a more intimate relationship with the passage of time. Our created references allow us to reminisce about the harvests of years before.

The benefits of 'green juices' are renowned. Your Smart Garden can become your green juice supercentre. Gemma and I juice whole beets for breakfast, leaves and all. It presents us with myriad health and wellness benefits, and we are utilising 100 per cent of the available plant material. There is no wasted part of produce that we have grown to provide nutrition for our bodies.

Like our other meals, green juices involve a family member perusing our garden aisles and selecting bits and pieces that they would like included in the juice. It is like shopping in your own personal living supermarket. It is a point of inspiration at the beginning of every meal preparation.

Part of your Smart Garden requirements must also include the security and the insurance it offers you and your family for whatever the future may hold. You may want to tuck it away somewhere in your yard and keep its existence relatively low-key. You may wish to have it, like we do, as an extension of the living area of our home and find security in its accessibility. It is something that will need to be part of your considerations. Suppose we were to see some level of societal breakdown, even for a short period. In that case, things like hunger can drive people to the point of desperation that may cause them to act in ways that would usually be considered unconscionable. There is only a certain level to which your garden can be protected, as even a bank can be robbed. Still, it is worth considering how you can at least make it the most secure it can be in the planning and design phase.

It is best to write down your dream list of requirements for your Smart Garden, start drawing mock garden bed designs and approximate the area you will need. As you go through this process, you will begin to see your Smart Garden take shape as many of your design improvements and opportunities will become self-evident. See over the page for an example.

It is also good practice to start recording planting maps and schedules. We use these to make sure we are maximising every square foot of our garden area. We can plan precisely where we want to plant the type of produce we want to be eating and log our successes and failures. This information becomes invaluable for plant rotation cycles and soil rebuilding and amendment programs.

Your Smart Garden ideas and concepts will initially nourish your dreams and fill your head. It will not be long before it becomes real, and then it can nourish and fill your belly as well!

Efficient Smart Garden Bed Design

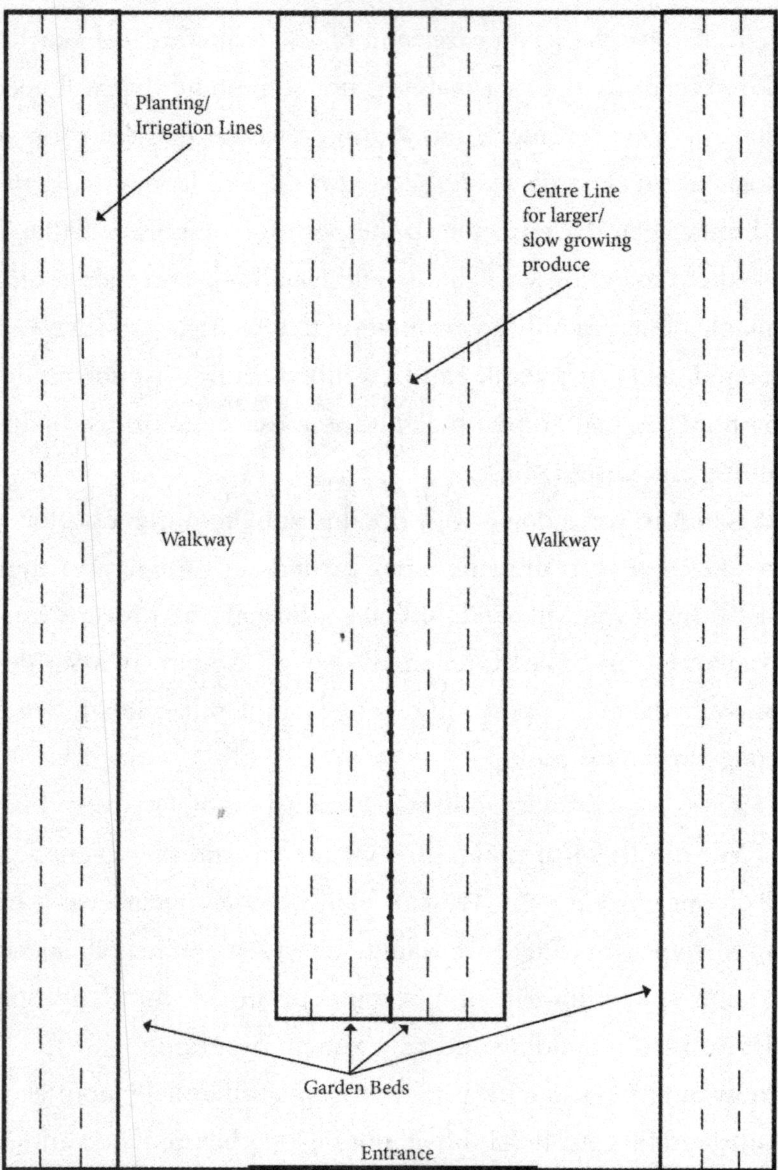

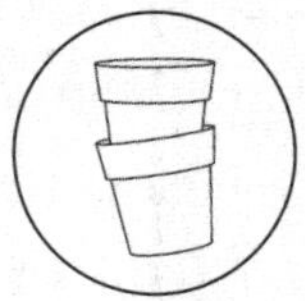

LET'S GET TECHNOGRARIAN

'Technology, like art, is a soaring exercise of the human imagination.'

– Daniel Bell, sociologist, writer and professor at Harvard University

To incorporate the technograrian approach to your Smart Garden, you will need some essential tools and items. Below is a list of things we use to give us better yields and a healthier garden, and to reduce a lot of the guesswork and physical time needed to manage our garden. Each item will be further covered in its corresponding chapter below, but let's start with this overview of the what and why.

SOLAR-POWERED EXHAUST FANS

These are available at any hardware store or online. They are designed to automatically operate when the garden reaches a specific ambient temperature, usually at 28 degrees Celsius. Some premade greenhouses come with temperature-sensitive vent panels that will open automatically at similar temperatures. While these are great, they are not as effective as a fan-based system. On still days, trapped hot air will only slowly escape through these vents. Exhaust fans will draw out the hot air and purge it. You can calculate how much air the fan will draw out of your greenhouse by using the 'cubic feet per minute' rating of the fan. Our system can purge all the air in the garden out through the fans in about 40 minutes, meaning all the air in the garden has now been recycled. They will also create beneficial air currents within the garden, and pesky birds cannot enter through the exhaust fans.

BRIX METER

A Brix meter is an invaluable part of any technograrian approach to Smart Gardening. In simple terms, a Brix meter measures the sugar content of the liquid from crushed plant material. It measures the refracted light that is visible through the liquid. You simply need to squeeze some juice out of, say, a spinach leaf into the Brix meter and then hold it up to the light. You will then see a number appear on the digital display on the meter. The higher the number, the higher the natural sugar levels of the plant juice.

Brix meters were first used in the wine industry to help viticulturists determine the best time to harvest their grapes, when their natural sugar content peaked. While not precisely indicative of nutrient content, higher natural sugar levels in plant material can be a guide for higher nutrient density. As I have already mentioned, it is interesting that when we eat super-healthy fresh produce, a recurring comment made is that it tastes 'sweet'. I can't help but believe that our body's 'sweet' perception is an innate biological acknowledgement of higher nutritional value. I also wonder if that isn't a driving force in the sugar addiction that plagues our society.

Every year we endeavour to attain higher Brix scores for our produce than we did the year before. For example, if we measure store-bought spinach and achieve a Brix score of 3 and then test our Smart Garden grown version, and it achieves a score of 12, it is not unreasonable to assume our homegrown produce is nutritionally far superior. The problem with a Brix meter is that you could add sugar to water and measure that and achieve a very high score. Obviously, a sugar/water solution contains little nutritional value. So, your results need to be tempered.

A Brix meter does give us a guiding line in the sand, though, and annual increases in Brix scores is a great goal to set yourself. It also makes for illuminating discussion with friends and family when measuring their store-bought items with your homegrown items.

HYGROMETERS

Hygrometers are a cheap and effective way to measure the ambient temperature and relative humidity inside your Smart Garden. Temperatures that are too high or humidity that is too high or too low can be very detrimental to your garden. A hygrometer will help you see what is happening inside your garden from one moment to the next.

We have used hygrometers in our garden to isolate 'hot spots' where heat is layering. That information can be used to know where to place an exhaust fan. Also, we use our hygrometer to tell us how often and for how long we need to automate our overhead misting system. We aim to maintain about 50 per cent relative humidity, and a simple overhead misting system achieves that. We only run our misting system hourly for a few minutes through the middle of the day, and it works a treat.

LIQUID FERTILISER SPRAY PACK

These again come in a variety of shapes, sizes and costs. The simplest is a hand-pump version that you add your liquid fertiliser to and then use the attached spray arm and nozzle to apply a fine misting spray to your plants. There are also electric ones now available that dispense with the need to hand-pump pressure into the unit. These are great but can be expensive.

Regular foliar and microbial soil spraying is a vital part of your technograrian approach to increase plant health and yields and shorten harvest timeframes.

ELECTRON MICROSCOPE

A 400x electron microscope is a very cost-effective way for you to get a firsthand view of the fascinating world of soil microbes. While you do not need to scientifically identify every critter that appears on your microscope screen, seeing and measuring increases in microbial activity and numbers is a sure sign you are on the right track with your garden care and maintenance.

These microscopes are relatively simple units and can be purchased easily online. It may sound a bit repetitive, but the reality is that everything we do in our Smart Garden is focused on increasing the microbial numbers and activity in our soil. Being able to see this firsthand is unbelievably inspiring and insightful. Growing abundant, nutrient-dense food is our goal, and our microbes are the key that unlocks the path of the minerals in our soil to our plants.

COMPOST TEA BREWER

The ability to create compost teas and microbial solutions is also an essential part of your technograrian approach. While compost teas are not a new concept, the way and ease in which you can make them has improved markedly over the last few years. Many compost tea brewers are available on the market, from simple bucket-based kits to advanced, highly technological units. I found the kits to be of great value compared to buying the parts individually and building them yourself. Often the kits will come with fertiliser and microbial starter packs to get you going as well.

You can buy many different types of great liquid fertiliser products off the shelf at gardening and hardware stores. These can negate the need for you to create your fertiliser solutions at home, but having a tea brewer on hand would be highly desirable if these became unavailable.

SOIL-TESTING KIT

Investment in a good soil-testing kit is an essential asset to your garden. A soil-testing kit can give you insight into high or low pH levels in your soil. More advanced versions can also indicate certain mineral deficiencies. While home testing kits fall well short of a laboratory-based soil test, they are an excellent way to help get things set up, at least initially, when you are in the first few years of your garden lifecycle.

Historically denoting 'potential of hydrogen', pH is the unit of measurement for the acidity or alkalinity of a substance. A plant's ability to take up nutrients, and indeed what nutrients are available in the soil, are affected by its pH level. Most plants prefer slightly acidic soil as this gives them access to the greatest range of available nutrients.

We found pH levels tended to vary more in the early days of our garden. When you first get your soil delivered to your garden, it will take a while to settle down, which will be reflected in the plants you grow. The more you add varied inputs to your soil, the more it will naturally balance itself out. A soil-testing kit can also show you that balance taking place as your test results become less varied and start to resolve themselves.

BIOLOGICAL PEST CONTROL

Pests will invade your garden from time to time. Whitefly, aphids and spider mites are just a few of the problems that can occur with any garden. Again, like the pH levels in our soil, the longer we build the overall health of our garden, the less we have any incidence of pests or disease.

Biological pest control is using predatory insects to control an infestation of unwanted insects. In the second year of our Smart Garden, we had an infestation of whitefly. While we used some organic pest control methods with mixed success, we could see that we were fighting a losing battle. Many of these infestations are seasonal, but the lifecycle of many problematic garden insects often involves them hibernating in the soil over winter, only to re-emerge in spring when temperatures warm again.

We realised we needed to find a new way to manage this outbreak. We contacted a biological pest control company and explained our problem to them. They suggested we try two types of tiny wasps that feed on the whitefly larvae. Once a week, we would pick up a small container of these wasps from our local post office and place them around our garden. We were amazed that the whitefly had all but disappeared within a few weeks as the tiny wasps took to work.

So, we bought a farm in Tassie, rainbows included!

Setting up all of the upright poles for the garden.

Adding exterior wall cross braces to attach the Laserlite sheeting to.

The start of the roofing sections with some 6000 roofing screws!

The garden starts to take shape but looks more like a horse arena!

All the family is on deck. Laying weed matting ready for the pine mulch walkways.

First garden bed construction begins. They look very shiny and new.

Gemma's on the barrow . . . it's that Italian work ethic!

No one is safe from helping, including young boys on sleepovers!

This was to become our seed propagation room, but we found that the actual garden beds germinate seeds really well without this step.

Second bed is now done and full of old timber. Just waiting on some fresh soil.

This is the doorway from our living room to our veggie patch. Every day we open the doors and are hit with a lovely warmth and amazing smells!

Almost done, and ready for the first loads of soil to be added to the beds.

We wanted to create the largest area of garden beds possible given the size of the garden structure.

With 30 acres of forest on our farm, there was plenty of fallen timber we could use.

These wood rounds will act as a water reservoir for the soil above.

Using wood in the bottom of the garden beds offers several benefits.

Our '*Hügelkultur*' raised garden beds are finally finished. We have used arsenic-free treated pine in the garden but still wrapped the centre posts in Laserlite to make sure there was no soil contact.

We scattered lime to help with wood decomposition and also added complex mineral additives before the soil went in.

A heavy wheelbarrow and a steep ramp . . . this will be fun.

The beautiful chocolate-brown soil looks great against the steel and timber.

Gemma adds the special 'hand smooth' touches and our first bed is almost complete.

Done!

Trialling a 12-week 'living supermarket' concept.

Choosing seeds for your garden planting is half the fun.

This is a good example of 'stagger planting' your produce. Through spring and summer, we will remove entire plants that are ready to harvest and replace them with new seeds or seedlings.

Living with the natural cycles with your own veggie patch is a blessing.

You can almost hear all the growing going on!

The best place for a coffee and a good (gardening) book!

Carrots highlight the importance of having deep garden beds and friable (not compacted) soils.

First sweet potato trial, an outstanding success!

Vine-ripened and just beginning to turn red.

Asian greens are so easy to grow and prolific in a Smart Veggie Patch. You will always have a meal at your fingertips.

Perfect start to a homegrown Italian feast.

Gemma makes a bottled crushed garlic that is OMG!

Happiness is . . . a table full of family and freshly picked food.

When the eggplants are pumping we make and freeze truckloads of moussaka for yummy winter dinners.

Slow-roasted fresh garden tomatoes add another layer of flavour.

All hands on deck for the post-harvest prep.

Fresh basil, eggplant and spring onions are ready to be sautéed for our secret family pasta sauce blend.

Ahhh, the smell of this year's cucumber pickles being made.

As parents we always want what is best for our kids. Providing them with nutritious, organic food every day of their young lives is the best place to start, and a Smart Veggie Patch is the best classroom there is.

By breaking the lifecycle of the whitefly, they managed to control the outbreak in a very quick time. Best of all, it did not involve the use of any chemicals or toxic preparations.

Once the whitefly was under control, the wasps naturally died out until just a tiny colony remained, ready to spring into action again in the coming spring. Since then, we have never again had an issue with whitefly. We know of other growing facilities that have not used the biological mitigation approach and have been rendered inoperable by whitefly in the past.

(It is worth mentioning that our first response to most of the new developments we might find in our garden, such as the emergence of pests, is to see if the garden will naturally respond and rebalance the situation itself. In the early days, we were more likely to freak out and jump to action. Over the years, we have realised that the vast majority of potential problems in the garden will have a way of fixing themselves. We now always err on this holistic style of mitigation. It also promotes natural environmental predators or plant responses to manage the situation. This ultimately builds a more resilient, healthier garden that requires less intervention and input on our behalf.)

DIGITAL IRRIGATION CONTROLLER

As I have stated already, your Smart Garden irrigation system has the most significant impact in improving the output and health of your garden and reducing your workload. In their simplest form, they are a manual switch that can turn your water system on and off at set times of the day. In large-scale protected cropping facilities, they can control hundreds of different irrigation lines (called stations) and work in tandem with real-time environmental data.

Your irrigation controller can be set up to turn any of your stations on and off, multiple times in one day. It can also be used to apply seasonal variations to those settings. For example, you can set it up to automatically water your garden more in summer and less in winter. You can also set it up to only water on odd or even days of the month, and it can tell you how much water has been used by different stations and their overall usage. The latest controllers can also be solar-powered, which is great for your garden's off-grid functionality.

For a typical Smart Garden design, a four-station unit would work best. That would allow you to set up stations one and two for the outside beds, and station three would be your centre bed. I would use station four as a misting system controller for the summer months. You can purchase a four-station controller at any hardware store or garden centre. Depending on how technologically adept you are, it could be worth having your system set up by an irrigation expert. Once installed, your irrigation controller will offer years of trouble-free operation.

Sufficient soil moisture content is critical to creating truly healthy soil, and hand-watering your garden is incredibly time inefficient. Our goal with a Smart Garden is maximum food output for minimal time input. There are many more important things you can be doing with your precious time. Consistency is vital when it comes to your Smart Garden. Having a reliable automated system that is watering your garden at specific times and year-round is essential.

The products above represent what I believe are the core items needed to create your Smart Garden. Our ultimate goal is to create a food production system. What each of these products brings to your garden is greater insight into real-time data and efficiency. I am sure some of you are probably thinking, 'Gee, do I need all this? I just want to make a garden for my family.' Well, there does often seem to be a disconnect between people's garden goals and realities. Most garden projects come to their demise because people do not truly appreciate the time and effort they require. A Smart Garden is about using science and technology to reduce the time and effort needed, increasing the amount and quality of what you produce and being an independent sustainable system. These attributes ultimately improve your chances of long-term success and create a garden that will become your pride and joy.

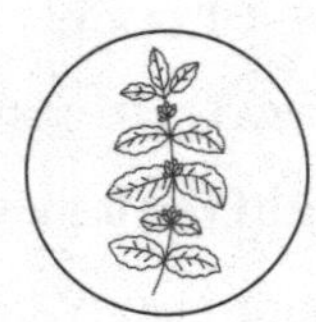

STEP 1: DESIGNING YOUR SMART GARDEN DREAM

The first aspect of your Smart Garden design you need to consider is its position relative to the sun. You will need to place it where you are achieving maximum sunlight hours and direct sunlight exposure. Shadow from other buildings or trees can cover gardens for extended periods throughout the day and these will produce far less than a fully sunlit garden. Pay particular attention to winter sun patterns. In winter, your Smart Garden can produce large amounts of food. With shorter sunlight hours through the day, you need to have it placed in a position that maximises all available sunlight. Soil temperature is critical for seed germination, so sunlight needs to be available to warm the soil. You can use other methods to warm the soil, but the sun is the easiest and most energy-efficient.

Depending on whether you live in a cold or hot location, you can decide the best way to minimise your site's negative aspects. Shade cloth can be used in areas with too much heat and direct sunlight in summer as this can burn and dehydrate the foliage and fruit of your plants. Plants that are suffering heat stress will yield far less. A plant will be heat-stressed well before visual indications of wilting and yellowing appear. Smart Gardens designed for colder climates allow you to close off the area and retain as much heat as possible. There always needs to be a steady flow of air through the garden. Insects such as bees must have access to the garden. Wall and roof areas covered in larger diameter mesh will allow them easy access.

With the ever-decreasing size of backyards, finding a space suitable for your Smart Garden can be challenging. For an average family, we believe that an area of approximately 5 metres x 5 metres represents a garden size capable of producing enough fresh produce for at least 70 per cent of the family needs. With a total area of 25 square metres (or 260 square feet), it is not a problematic allocation of space to make, even if your yard area is on the smaller side.

Many companies offer 'off the shelf' greenhouses that can be modified to suit the protected Smart Garden methodology. While they are available in various lengths, the width of the greenhouse is usually limited. We suggest you get the widest greenhouse you can find, as this allows for more workspace in between the garden beds contained inside. The walkways between your garden beds need to be wide enough for you to manoeuvre an average-sized wheelbarrow between them easily.

When creating garden walkways, they need to have both an entry and an exit point or a large turning circle area. This helps you avoid the need to walk backwards while pulling a fully laden wheelbarrow and therefore creating a trip hazard. While you want to maximise your garden bed area, if your walkways are too narrow, you will also run the risk of hitting your hands against the beds while manoeuvring items like your trusty wheelbarrow in and around them.

Depending on the height of your garden beds, you also need to consider the potential roof height if you wish to grow taller plants and vegetables. Vegetables like broad beans and certain varieties of tomatoes can grow incredibly tall. Over the years, we have moved to shorter 'bush' varieties of these types of plants. We have found harvesting problematic when it becomes difficult to access the plants' tops from a standing position. While sometimes the use of ladders and other elevated work surfaces is unavoidable, we try to minimise their use as they represent a fall hazard.

A minimum ceiling height of 3 metres will work well for a variety of reasons. One is the ability for heated air to move higher and therefore further away from the plants growing in the garden, and also for the potential placement of ceiling-mounted misting systems to help control the garden's humidity without drowning the plants below.

You may have noticed that the ceiling or roof height of commercial greenhouses and protected cropping environments can be incredibly high, depending on the plant and crop varieties growing within them. As plants are very prone to heat stress, we want to raise ambient temperatures while making sure we do not elevate temperatures to a point where they become detrimental. It is also prudent to check with local councils and government on regulations that might dictate maximum roof heights for ancillary buildings in your city or town.

Your protected Smart Garden can be a standard pergola-type structure that offers a roof covering for your garden in its simplest form. You can then harvest the water from the roof area and use the structure to attach shade cloth or irrigation lines. We would suggest at least one solid wall that can protect your garden from the worst of the prevailing winds. Use local weather information on wind directions to assess which side of your garden will be most susceptible to the prevailing winds.

If you are lucky enough not to have an issue with predator pests like possums, then you can afford to leave some sides of your garden open. It is worth mentioning one overlooked problem that can arise from having a semi-open protected garden, particularly in a suburban environment. Often cats will foul in the fresh soil of garden beds if given a chance. This can be particularly dangerous for pregnant women and people with compromised immune systems as it can contain a parasite called *Toxoplasma gondii*. This parasite can cause toxoplasmosis, and it is a common but potentially dangerous disease.

Having a Smart Garden that is fully enclosed does have advantages. Birds can also become a problem in an open-sided garden, as can pests like rats. We negate these issues by replacing some solid wall panels with mesh inserts. The mesh is small enough to prevent these larger animals from accessing the garden while being large enough for fresh air, bees and insects to move freely in and out.

We also suggest you try and place your garden as close to your home's living areas as you can – although individual circumstances, such as availability of sunlight, might not make placing your garden near your home possible. In Europe, the concept of a 'kitchen garden' started in France. It was generally a herb and vegetable garden that was either a walled garden joined to the kitchen or easily accessed from the kitchen. Their benefits are numerous.

Your Smart Garden will be more easily used, cared for and maintained if it is somewhere that makes interaction easy. When your garden is close to your home, it also makes it more secure from predators . . . of all types! During meal preparation, being able to grab a knife and quickly harvest a fresh bounty from your garden makes you far more likely to do so. Even when your garden is part of your home, it is easy to forget during the busyness of life that you have a garden full of nutritious produce just waiting to be eaten. A great way to think about your Smart Garden is as an extension of your kitchen and a living fresh produce pantry for you and your family.

STEP 2: GET SMART ABOUT SOIL

As with many of the topics I am covering in the last part of this book, soils and garden beds could easily be a book in itself. I aim to give you direction and advice on achieving the healthiest soil and a garden bed design that is cheap, practical and functional. In this chapter, we will look at the easiest and most cost-effective way you can achieve excellent soil health for your garden and essential things to look out for and avoid.

Advanced scientific knowledge of soil science is already explored in many books. It is an area of research that is growing at an exponential rate. I have found it fascinating in my exploration in and around soil science that the information we know seems to change and dramatically increase every few months. When attending a soil health workshop, we will often be informed by the instructor that the information we learned last year is now outdated and new information is available.

Many people struggle with the existing soils they find in their backyard. Very rarely are these soils appropriate for growing fresh vegetables and herbs. I have seen gardeners struggling with dry clay-based powdered soil that was void of organic material, microbial activity, and many nutrients and minerals. They stand there, peering down on their garden full of frustration and disappointment. Most backyard soils are not suitable for these reasons, but they can also contain toxic chemicals.

Often, we have no way of knowing if our home site was once factory land or farmland. The quiet remote dirt road we live on in Tasmania was once home to a thriving town. It had 28 houses, shops, churches, several coal mines and flourishing berry farms. Now there are just a few homes and the remnants of the mines.

Backyard soil will also contain many grass and weed seeds that will be a constant source of aggravation and work. Grass and weed seeds already in the soil will love all the nutrients, composts and amendments you will soon feed them. They will go crazy as you radically improve soil health to promote a flourishing high-yielding garden.

We have made this mistake ourselves and ended up creating weeds the likes of which we had never seen! Not only will you be actively promoting their growth, but you are also, in effect, making superweeds with incredible levels of resilience. We believe that using existing backyard soils for Smart Garden beds should be avoided for all the reasons above unless you are unable to get fresh soil from elsewhere.

You can purchase soil from several types of outlets, and it is worth approaching all your local soil suppliers for information about their products. Landscape centres will often stock a 'veggie mix' soil type. Local council waste refuse centres may also have soil for vegetable beds and gardens. One of the critical factors in finding the best soil available is finding out how long the soil has been composting.

The composting process kills grass and weed seeds within the soil due to the heat of decomposing material. The composting process also makes nutrients and minerals within the soil available to your plants. We have made the mistake of buying soil that was too 'green' or 'hot'. These terms describe soil that has not had sufficient time to break down and fully decompose. Complete decomposition needs to have occurred so plants can easily access all the goodies they need to promote their germination and provide an abundance of healthy fresh produce.

We have been frustrated by having to wait a further 12–18 months with nonproductive soil in our garden beds. It felt like an eternity before we started to see the results we had been aiming for. The longer the soil has been composting before you purchase it will significantly reduce the time you have to wait before your Smart Garden becomes the flourishing food production system you desire.

Local gardeners' knowledge is super helpful in finding out which suppliers' soil performs the best at any given time. Contact local seed sellers, garden stores and small-scale fresh produce suppliers. Often these people will know who is currently supplying the best performing soil. Due to composting timeframes, the supplier of the best available soil often changes. Different companies will be working up soils at different times, so it pays to ask around.

In Australia, we have standards governing the contents of commercial soil and their potential to contain seeds from grasses and weeds that can still germinate. So you will be purchasing soil that is virtually free of weeds and problem plants. Because we use this type of soil for our garden, we would spend on average less than 1 per cent of our time weeding. On the rare occasion we find a weed in our garden, it is often brought in by an outside source like birds or possums. Not having to weed your garden is a godsend and dramatically reduces your workload.

The 'organic' status and cleanliness of your soil is also essential. Making sure your soil is free of chemicals and toxic nasties is vitally important. This is where the council refuse soil can be problematic. Often these 'green waste' soils can be contaminated with plastics and other unwanted material. When digging around in our garden, we have had situations where we have unearthed small plastic pieces from the soil. It is not necessarily the pieces you can see that are the issue but the microplastics hidden in the soil. The larger pieces can be an indication that microplastics are also present. We inspect the soil closely to see if we can visually detect things that look like the soil may contain household or industrial waste.

While getting a soil analysis can be pretty costly, it is the only way you can be truly sure of what exactly you are starting with. A soil analysis will tell you what minerals are present in the soil and at what levels. A soil test is vital to determine if your soil is deficient in a mineral and needs rebalancing. This analysis can also detect things that you do not want in your garden soil, like heavy metals. We use an array of onsite soil-testing equipment that can give us an overview of the basics of the condition of our soils and use laboratory analysis when we need to establish a baseline from which to build on.

Many trace elements you need to create a super-healthy soil are not available with organic certification. Trace elements like cobalt or boron are a necessary ingredient of healthy soil, so they can become available for us to consume through the plants we eat. They are essential to human health but need to be consumed only at trace levels as they are toxic to us at high levels. A soil supplier who adds essential elements like a small amount of cobalt or boron to their composting soil mixes can automatically lose the 'certified organic' status for the soil, as both elements are chemicals. The nuances of the developing knowledge around soil science is one of the many areas that the broad brushstrokes of organic certification are unable to deal with. Again, discussions with your soil supplier will help you navigate around the need to find the cleanest, healthiest soil for your garden.

Even if the soil you eventually purchase is still a little too 'green' to effectively grow flourishing plants from the get-go, you can use foliar-applied amendments to feed your plants the minerals and nutrients your soil is not yet making available to them. We will look further at these types of sprays and amendments, but as with most potential problems with your Smart Garden, there are always ways you can mitigate issues as you face them.

Perhaps this is why the knowledge of longtime gardeners is so valuable. While our Smart Garden design and technograrian methods avoid many of the usual garden issues and pitfalls, every garden is a unique microcosm unto itself. It is a living community made up of trillions and trillions of organisms trying to build communities and thrive. To help explain just how complex soil science can be, here is a remarkable and well-known fact when it comes to your typical healthy garden soil – there are more living things and lifeforms within a handful of soil than the number of all the people who have lived or ever will live on planet Earth!

So, of course, you will always face some battles and challenges getting these balances right.

Your soil is the foundation and engine room for your garden. There is no more important aspect for you to consider. Even the most beautifully designed and fully automated Smart Garden will only ever be as good as the soil in its garden beds. We have learned over the years that of all the time and effort we spend tending our garden, more than half is devoted to improving and rebuilding our soil. It is the critical difference between us getting no harvest, or some harvest, to a good harvest, and then an incredible-tasting, nutrient-dense, bountiful harvest. The knowledge we have gained with this hands-on approach made us realise that doing this on a large scale would be incredibly difficult. Intimately building soil over many hundreds of acres would be extremely time and labour intensive. This is why industrial farming needs to use so many chemical short cuts.

You can build terrible base soils into something better, but it takes time . . . lots of time! As all organic matter, minerals and nutrients you have added begin to break down, slowly, the microbial populations will begin to build. Find a local soil supplier that has at least done most of this work for you. In that case, your Smart Garden will have a running start to produce a rich bounty for you and your family from the outset.

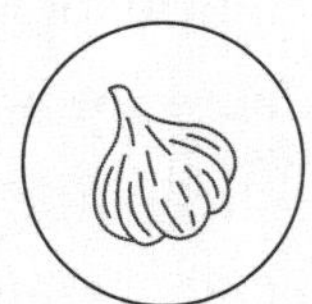

STEP 3: GARDEN BED DESIGN

We have used several different garden bed designs, from typical ground-level beds to elaborate raised beds. Your garden beds' design is a critical component to the overall success of your garden as they can be problematic in many different ways. Without delving into the pros and cons of individual styles, I will explain how to build what I believe to be the most cost-effective and functional.

The height of a raised bed needs to allow you easy access to the soil work area. A bed that is too low will be the source of sore backs, and you do not want to be overly stooped as you prepare soils and plant seeds. An excellent average starting height will be 80 centimetres (32 inches). This height works well, as a lot of off-the-shelf panelling or siding you can use for your beds comes in standard 200-millimetre (8-inch) widths. That means you could use a treated pine wood panel with a standard length of 2400 millimetres x 200 millimetres

(94 inches x 8 inches). If we stack four of these panels on top of each other long ways, it will give us the 800 millimetres we require.

As Gemma and I are on the taller side of the average height, we have corrugated tin panels for the sides of our garden beds. This is very easy to install but lacks some structural rigidity, and these beds can quickly end up having quite pronounced bowing along their sides.

Timber uprights can be easily attached to a steel fence post or picket in the corners and where the panels meet in the garden beds. These are usually called a 'T post' or a 'Y post'. You then hammer these manually into the ground with a mallet, large hammer or steel post driver. If using a mallet or a hammer, I suggest you place some hardwood on top of the post before you begin to hammer it into the ground and hit the wood, not the steel picket. I have found that hammering the steel post directly can cause razor-sharp edges and burrs, and these can be exposed in your garden. Using the wood to buffer the impact between your hammer and your picket will prevent damage and give you a larger surface area to strike.

You can also purchase a steel post driver, a large metal cylinder with handles on the side that slides over the post and is used to drive it into the ground. They are a worthwhile purchase as not only do they reduce the chance of the steel post forming sharp edges, they also make it much easier to maintain a 90-degree angle on your post and keep it on a straight, upright trajectory. Another handy tip for avoiding the chance of injuries from posts is to top them off with plastic caps for steel posts, which you can purchase from any local hardware store. They are usually bright yellow and help attract bees!

Ultimately, the materials you use to build your garden beds are only limited by your imagination. Here are a couple of tips I would suggest you take into consideration with your design:

- Beds that are 60 centimetres (24 inches) wide are a great size to work with, as they do not require too much leaning forward to reach produce. They can also be effectively covered by two irrigation driplines running at 15-centimetre and 45-centimetre spacing. Also, most plant spacing requirements call for 30 centimetres between plants in your garden bed.
- If you are using pressure-treated wood that will have direct soil contact, make sure you choose an arsenic-free variety. Standard CCA (copper, chromium and arsenic) timber could potentially leach arsenic or chromium into your soil, so make sure you ask for the ACQ (alkaline copper quarternary) version.
- Timber sleepers can be a great garden bed building material. Avoid old timber that has been used as railway sleepers as they can contain fine traces of asbestos dust from the brake pads of trains.
- Using recycled material is a terrific idea. A bit of imagination and a trip to your local waste disposal centre can inspire some excellent garden bed designs. Again, be aware of potential toxic issues with things you find. Gemma and I once found a bunch of old brightly coloured steel roof panels that would have made great garden walls, only to realise they had been painted in lead-based paint!
- Our garden bed design incorporated *Hügelkultur* principles. In hindsight, we should not have made them quite so wide, as reaching taller plants in the middle requires quite a bit of stretching.
- Our garden bed design was simple and cost-effective. By creating an understorey of wood, we saved on soil cost and increased the temperature of the soil, and the wood also helps the beds hold water.

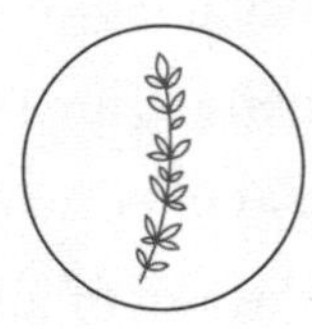

STEP 4: THINK IRRIGATION AND AUTOMATION

Watering a garden by hand is the common mistake that we all seem to make when we begin our gardening journey. Along with soil choice, watering is the most crucial aspect in creating your Smart Garden. For soil to be at its best, it needs to contain approximately 30–40 per cent water. Water also makes up 85–95 per cent of the weight of growing plants, and it is the water that carries soil nutrients to the plant so they can be absorbed.

Plants that have access to their required water needs will be much healthier and more robust. Many people like the interaction of hand-watering their plants with either a hose or watering can. It is a great way to tour your garden and feel a direct connection to what is growing. Still, it is often the first place we fall short when our time-pressured lives see us not getting around to our daily water regime.

Our garden's system is fed by a water tank that we fill from a freshwater spring on our farm. The tank is up on a hill, so gravity supplies the water pressure for the irrigation lines. When we first started gardening, we would need to find the time to hand-water the garden every day. Even with the best of intentions, time would get away from us with the busy lifestyle of having a farm and many young children. Several days could go past without the garden getting watered, to detrimental effect!

It was often not until we saw the telltale signs of dehydration and withering plants that we would then go out and usually overwater our garden to restore some vitality to the plants. Plants that grow in this environment are much less likely to flourish. They need to biologically operate very differently from a plant that always has an abundance of water on tap (pun intended!).

It highlights one of the essential premises in creating a genuinely bountiful garden. You want to create an environment for your plants in your Smart Garden that represents a mini-Utopia. A plant can only truly thrive if it believes its most important biological imperative, survival, is absolutely ensured. Your plants need to believe that they do not have to worry about storing water or nutrients. They also need to know that they do not have to keep their plant mass smaller to not waste energy. A plant that feels threatened will not fruit or produce as much volume. A plant that is in purely survival mode is not going to flourish.

We see many gardens where the plants are just in survival mode. The soil is mineral- and nutrient-deficient, and the plants do not have access to sufficient water, so they are never fully expressing their potential vitality. Think of the difference in feelings and attitude you have when you find yourself in an environment where you are not sure of your safety compared to a place where you feel totally secure.

Your Smart Garden needs to be the place of ultimate safety for your plants. We have seen some amazing reactions from plants to our 'safe place' garden. We can now have year-round tomato plants! We have had some tomato plants be so disease-free and so happy, they continued to grow throughout a cold Tasmanian winter and jump-started a new year in spring already full of flowers.

Due to their perceived lavish setting, plants decide that this is a great place to be and therefore flourish. We benefit from them producing for many more weeks and months outside a traditional season. Our garden then becomes far more economically viable, valuable and sustainable. Perhaps if we can keep improving our little Utopia even further, some other traditional garden rules may no longer apply. Our seasonal plants may develop the potential to become year-round producers, or at least vastly extend their seasonality.

I only highlight these findings to emphasise the importance of watering your garden. Those missed days and weeks will only throw your plants into survival mode, and they will never produce a harvest worthy of the time and effort you have spent to create your Smart Garden in the first place. We have learned the hard way that the only way you can ensure your garden always has a sufficient water supply is by installing an automated irrigation system.

There are many different styles and types of garden irrigation systems, and all have specific strong and weak points. We suggest a dripline system that runs along the top of your beds in lines about 20–30 centimetres apart. The reasons we recommend this are several-fold. A drip system is the most efficient use of your precious water supply. As the soil immediately absorbs the drops of water from the lines, it significantly reduces the water's evaporation and the wetted area in the soil below is tear- or pear-shaped. The water is then available to provide the most benefit to the plant's root system.

These irrigation driplines produce a specific amount of water at each point so you can calculate how much water is supplied over a particular timeframe. They come in various sizes, thicknesses and drip point frequencies. Drip points approximately 20–30 centimetres apart will give you great coverage for your garden. By calculating how much water is supplied, you can exactly replicate a perfect day, week and year's worth of typical rainfall for your area.

Our driplines are also 'compensated', which means that the same amount of water comes out of every drip point. Uncompensated driplines will supply more water at the far ends of the lines than near the top, so we prefer compensated lines.

A quick word of warning about some dripline or 'soaker' products sold on the market. As we found out many years ago with our research into irrigation systems, some of these products are made from recycled tyres. The rubber in tyres is highly toxic and is why they are treated as their own category at waste refuse centres. Some council refuse centres will not even accept them at all. When tyres are recycled into another product, they go through a process that can make them many times more toxic than the original tyres due to the chemicals and compounds needed to break them down.

We found label warnings on some irrigation hoses that stated they contained 'known carcinogens'. Using products that carried warnings like 'do not drink from this hose as it contains known carcinogens' in our organic chemical-free garden seemed counter-intuitive. We discussed this with several organic certification bodies. We were surprised to find that many had no policy or position in using these products in an organically certified garden. Suffice it to say, we did not use these products and constantly check the fine print on anything we are bringing into our Smart Garden.

A timer unit controls our irrigation driplines to turn them on and off during specific times of the day and night and govern the length of time they are on for. These units are available off the shelf at any local hardware store and range from simple manual timers that can control a single tap outlet to digital timers that can be operated from an app on your phone. These control multiple electrically operated solenoids that turn the system on and off and can even compensate for days of rain or temperature increases.

We prefer driplines over spray-type points as many plants suffer from being always wet. Tomatoes are much more prone to disease if constantly wet, as are many types of lettuce and other vegetables. Drip systems apply water to the soil, where it is needed most. It is still highly desirable to give your plants regular topical watering. Without the natural mechanisms of wind and rain to help remove expelled toxins and waste build-up on the leaves of your plants, it is a way you can make sure they stay in prime condition. By giving them a vigorous weekly watering, you help remove those toxins and clean the plant's natural filtration systems. And you get your fix of pleasurable hand-watering time in your garden.

I have no scientific reasoning for this but have always felt that vigorous watering also enlivens plants and could be responsible for triggering them to set their root systems a bit deeper and more robustly. This may be in response to them being buffeted around a little bit by the water pressure. Our plants often remind us of our kids in summer playing under the hose when we water them – all gleaming and alive with excitement and energy.

In real terms, our irrigation system was an investment in our garden. It represented the fourth-largest cost in creating our Smart Garden, after the costs of the actual building structure, soil and our garden beds. As watering the garden is something we could do ourselves, it felt like it represented a garden design's luxury aspect. How wrong we were!

Suppose we were to apportion our garden's success to the many specific aspects that contribute to it. In that case, our irrigation system is at least 30 per cent of the reason we enjoy such bountiful harvests and the freedom of a) not having to water the garden daily and b) not feeling bad because we forgot to water our garden. Investment in an irrigation system will quickly pay itself off in the first year or two of your Smart Garden's life.

I am not sure why, but many people seem reluctant to invest in a quality irrigation system or make some token effort with some uncompensated piping and the odd (generally clogged) spray point. With a bit of planning and discussions with your local irrigation supplier, you can quickly build and design an effective system yourself, or many companies will install the system for you.

In Tasmania, we have seen many new irrigation companies and businesses start operating as demand from both commercial and residential customers increases. While we are always looking for ways to reduce the cost of creating your Smart Garden, investment into a fully automated irrigation system will always be money very well spent.

The final piece in the irrigation and automation system of your Smart Garden will be how you harvest and manage your water supply. One of the key benefits of building your protected garden space is your ability to gather the rainfall from the roof area of your Smart Garden. This then allows you to specifically target this water to your garden beds using your irrigation system. Your Smart Garden becomes self-sufficient in relation to its water requirements. Better still, you avoid using town or local water supplies that can be relatively expensive and may contain chemicals like chlorine and fluoride. Even rainwater that is harvested in areas that may be exposed to airborne pollutants can be filtered before you use it in your garden.

STEP 5: RAIN HARVESTING AND WATER STORAGE

Your Smart Garden acts as an excellent rain harvesting structure that allows you to capture rain runoff from the roof and use the water for your garden. You will need to make sure that your structure has a guttering system and purchase a tank capable of holding enough water to get you through the driest parts of the weather pattern in your area.

If you multiply the rainfall by your roof area, you will figure out how many litres of water you can harvest in a year. For example, on our farm, we average 600 millimetres of rain a year, and our Smart Garden roof area is 200 square metres. So we can calculate using 600 x 200 = 120,000. This means we potentially harvest 120,000 litres of rainwater per year from our roof.

Our rainfall pattern varies over a year, but August is our wettest month, with 63 millimetres of average rainfall. Suppose we use our simple calculation again and include the potential rainfall figure, for example. In that case, 63 x 200 = 12,600, which shows we could collect more than 12,000 litres of water during August alone. As we know how many metres of irrigated dripline we have in the garden and how many minutes it is irrigating per day, we can also calculate how much we are likely to use.

Suppose we use our standard 25-square-metre Smart Garden design and assume an average of 600 millimetres of rain per year. In that case, our rainfall capture potential is 15,000 litres per year or approximately 1250 litres per month. We can calculate our water usage because we know that the two irrigation lines of 13-millimetre dripline with 30-centimetre spacings (the distance between the drip holes) will emit 1.6 litres of water for every hour they are on. This means that we would use about 1250 litres per month if we automated our irrigation system to run for five minutes every morning and night.

I believe a water storage tank that could hold between 2000 and 3000 litres of water would be ideal for this scenario. Tanks of this size come in a range of shapes and designs. Having the extra holding capacity means you can store water in the good times for use in the drier times. A small solar-powered water pump can be used to supply the water to the irrigation system. The system is then not reliant on power from the electricity grid.

Another benefit is that you will have extra drinking water for use in your home should your town water supply be affected in any way. This ability to effectively capture and redistribute water is one of the significant benefits of a Smart Garden. Not only is it the epitome of self-sufficiency, but it is also an incredibly effective use of resources.

If there was one aspect that we see in many other gardens that really reduces their yield potential and the garden's overall health, it is a lack of moisture in the soil. Having a free water source from rain means you never have to think twice about using water for your garden. Better still, having an automated irrigation system means you rarely have to think about it at all!

STEP 6: WHAT TO PLANT?

When it comes to all the amazing fruits and vegetables you can plant, you are ultimately only limited by your imagination. Predictably the first motivator in your choice will be growing the food you love to eat! Look at the fresh produce you would typically purchase in your weekly grocery shop and see what would be the easiest to begin growing in your Smart Garden.

It is also fun to offer all family members the option to make suggestions on what they might like to see in the family's Smart Garden. Often, we will let our children choose their seeds or seedlings from local suppliers and plant them themselves. It is always fascinating to watch how much ownership of the plants' care and management they take on and the delight they feel when the family sits down to a meal of 'their' carrots or broccoli. It shows them that they can produce food for themselves, which also helps build resilience and independence.

Recently our youngest son chose a variety of kale that we had never considered. It grew into a bountiful plant, producing a massive amount of lovely dark green and nutrient-rich foliage. After his first harvest, we could not believe how fantastic this new variety tasted. It has now become the primary variety we use in our garden.

Other things to consider and factors that now affect our plant choices are times to harvest, edible percentages, soil impact, nutritional value and harvestability.

Some vegetables can take many months until they are ready for harvest and therefore take up valuable garden bed space while growing. Many of the same vegetables are also cheap to purchase from other growers or are not necessarily a great source of nutrients. For this reason, we do not usually grow plants like onions in our beds.

Onions are cheap and easy to buy, and although they add great flavour and texture to many different meals, they are not, by comparison, a great source of vitamins and minerals. As they can also take many months to mature, it is not, in our opinion, worth growing them in our Smart Garden. We grow similar alternatives like spring onions and love the Red Legs variety, but these are fast-growing and take up little relative space. So, we suggest you assess vegetables you would like to grow in your garden based on the time from planting to harvest and their ability to convert your nutrient-rich soils into bioavailable nutrition for you and your family.

Another factor that dictates what we plant is the edible percentage of the fruit or vegetable we want to grow. With all the effort, time and cost it takes to build and maintain rich soil that is mineral- and nutrient-dense, we want to make sure that we can eat as much of the plant mass as possible. This serves many purposes. It makes the garden much more financially viable and maximises the reward of having your garden in the first place.

In the past, we have grown certain varieties of broccoli, cabbage and cauliflower and realised that the massive volume of inedible foliage they created had required them to draw a vast amount of nutrients from our soil. Those nutrients absorbed from the soil will now need to be replaced and for us, it did not represent an equitable use of those nutrient resources. Hopefully, your Smart Garden is a Utopic wonderland of magical plant love. If that is the case, the volume and size of everything you grow will be on the extreme side.

For us, the leaf size of cauliflowers grown in our garden are immense. After we have harvested a large round cauliflower head, typically, the remaining plant material can fill our average-sized wheelbarrow by itself! While the gathered cauliflower head is impressive, it would still only provide maybe two or three meal portions for our family. The cauliflower head would only represent around 20–25 per cent of the plant's total mass. The amount of nutrients and minerals drawn from the soil to grow and produce this prolific leaf size and volume must be replenished.

There is time, effort and financial cost in doing that. From our calculations, it does not represent an effective use of those resources. If we were to grow several beets in the same area, we would produce a vegetable that can have almost 100 per cent of the plant's mass consumed. We eat beet greens and the root, and we juice the entire plant as well in our green (now purple!) smoothies. We find we can use beetroots in everything from salads to baking, and most importantly, they are packed with vitamins and nutrients.

We have a rule of thumb when we look at what to plant in any given season. We like to aim for fruits and vegetables that, when harvested, offer at least 60 per cent or higher edible plant mass. This reduces the inedible by-product produced from our garden. We do not waste anything that grows in the garden. It will either go to feed chickens or other farm animals or be turned into compost. All of those processes are inefficient by comparison to our preferred 'pick it and eat it' scenario.

Another factor we always consider is the inherent nutritional value of a fruit or vegetable type. We have also seen and heard the dietician claims that we need to be consuming more colourful varieties of vegetables. Dr Michelle Hauser, a clinical fellow in medicine at Stanford Medical School and a chef and nutrition educator, advised:

> My response is simple: eat all of the colors of the rainbow . . . These colors signal the presence of diverse phytochemicals and phytonutrients. Phytochemicals and phytonutrients are beneficial substances produced by plants. People who eat diets rich in phytonutrients have lower heart disease rates and cancer – the two leading causes of death in the United States. As a bonus, vegetables provide fibre, which helps prevent constipation and helps keep cholesterol in check.[163]

You can find many reports and research articles on the internet about which fruits and vegetables provide the highest nutrition levels when consumed by humans. In our garden, we try to grow things that would best replicate what would be eaten as part of a typical Mediterranean diet.

The Mediterranean diet offers many health benefits and is thought to be a contributing factor in the long and active lives of people who predominantly eat in this manner. This diet was developed from their agrarian forebears in the small villages of southern Europe. It offers enormous optionality with recipes and meals that you can create. The fresh produce grown for this diet will also thrive in a protected cropping space like your Smart Garden, and your yields can far exceed your wildest expectations.

In our spring and summer plantings, we include lots of colourful vegetables like spinach, tomatoes, eggplant, beetroots and carrots, and herbs like oregano and basil. In autumn and winter, we move towards a more Asian theme with lots of fast-growing green leafy vegetables like bok choy and tatsoi, and supplement these with produce that we have stored and preserved from the previous spring/summer harvest.

The last factor we consider with plant choice is harvestability. In the past, we have tried many things that we found too fiddly or problematic for harvesting. This was usually because these plants simply grew too tall when planted in a raised garden bed. The other issue can be with plants that produce tiny fruits or edible parts that require you to go hunting to find them in a mass of foliage.

What seems to happen is that these plants are subconsciously avoided during quick pre-dinner harvest missions. It is often not until we remove the plant from the garden at the end of the season that we realise much of the plant's harvest has gone to waste. Finding beans to pick in a mass of foliage (with 52-year-old eyes!) is fun the first 20 times but can become a bit arduous after a while. This does not mean we do not plant beans, but we find smaller and easier varieties to search through.

This issue is, as our previous cauliflower example showed, the reality of a fully functioning Smart Garden's ability to produce a great mass of whatever you decide to plant. If your Smart Garden is created and maintained correctly, you will likely be dealing with plants that will be two or three times larger and more prolific than an average garden could produce. Our previously trialled green bean varieties ended up being several feet tall and several feet wide, and more than two feet thick through.

Plants that are growing in your Smart Garden environment can go crazy. Many seasoned gardeners walk into our garden and make comments like, 'Oh my goodness, I have never seen anything like it!'

We are often dealing with plant expressions that are way outside what a typical garden may produce. Although it is fantastic for your yields and harvest volume, it can also mean your garden can quickly become like an Amazonian jungle . . . or at least what it used to be.

Our beetroots can often weigh more than 1.5 kilograms each (2.7 kilograms is our record!), and our spinach leaves are well over 80 centimetres long and 30 centimetres wide. It is a testament to how much impact soil health and a protected environment has in producing incredible amounts of food. A word to the wise: we suggest choosing plants that you can manage easily and do not overwhelm you and your garden.

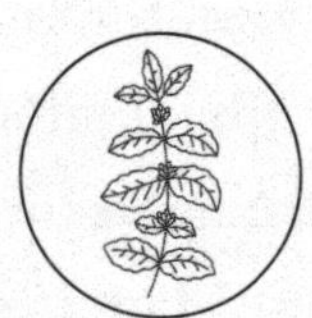

STEP 7: MICROBES – NATURE'S HIDDEN WORKERS

One of the most exciting areas of our garden for us is the soil. It is the engine room that makes all things possible. The science and emerging new research on how to best create soil that is nutrient and biologically rich is easily a book in itself. Every week we understand more about the incredibly complex symbiotic relationships between all the components that make up a living soil and its relationship to the plants it nourishes. I want to highlight two aspects of building exceptional nutrient-packed soil that has allowed us, over the years, to shorten the timeline to achieving flourishing bountiful harvests.

The realistic timeframe required for soils to build and balance themselves, given even the best of inputs, is still measured in months. As we covered in Step 2: Get Smart About Soil, a fully biologically available soil for plants needs to be at a certain point of decomposition. When this occurs, nutrients and minerals can be converted by microbes into forms that a plant can access and use.

Even today, there are pieces of the puzzle of exactly how all these microscopic interactions occur that we have not quite worked out yet. Good gardeners have known for quite a while now that lots of decomposing organic matter from various sources such as composts and manures will ultimately generate large populations of microbes that in turn feed nematodes. Microbes include viruses, bacteria, archaea, fungi, plants like algae, and protozoa, among other things.

For further information on the amazingly complex and fascinating lifecycles and interactions that occur in the billions in every handful of soil, it is worth researching the latest information on the Soil Food Web. The 'Invisiverse' is one term that I love. It depicts just how incredible this other world of microscopic lifeforms is.

Like the universe that we are a part of, the Invisiverse is astounding and awe-inspiring. As a complex natural system, we find that every part of the process is vitally important for the system's survival. Too little or too much of any aspect can throw the system out of balance. However, that balance is always ultimately restored; it just takes a long time for that to happen.

As we want our Smart Garden to be a food production system, we take our technograrian approach to kickstart this process by adding plenty of diverse decomposing organic material to our soil and by adding bacteria and microbes. We also use foliar sprays, which are liquids rich in nutrients and minerals that we spray directly onto the plants.

From our experience, if you started with an imported 'green' or 'hot' soil like we discussed earlier (one that is not very far along its decomposition process) and placed it in your garden beds, it would take approximately 2–3 years before it would be producing at the levels we aim for with our Smart Garden. Most people have well and truly given up on their home garden project long before this. We have heard many stories of gardens that initially did not produce and were abandoned, only to be restarted many years later and then delivered stunning results. The difference between garden attempt number one and number two is the lifecycle of the soil in action.

Applying large populations of healthy microbes to your garden requires you to grow them. Certain bacteria can be incredibly harmful to human beings, but many of them are profoundly beneficial. Every minute of every day, our bodies are exposed to billions of microbes and produce their own populations to help with many of our bodily systems.

With our Smart Garden, we use supercharged compost teas to increase the numbers of these beneficial microbes. They, in turn, get to work, converting nutrients into forms that our plants can consume and absorb. Fascinatingly, plants also perform many functions to support these microbes and help them grow in more significant numbers.

Microbes fall under two main categories: aerobic and anaerobic. Aerobic microbes need oxygen to survive, and anaerobic microbes do not need oxygen to survive. Microbes come in the form of bacteria, fungi, viruses and protozoa. Some dangerous bacteria, fungi and viruses can make people extremely ill, cause disease and even death. We are also exposed to billions of microbes that are either harmless or highly beneficial.

With our Smart Garden, we want to promote a healthy type of microbe and avoid harmful types. When working with microbes, it is always crucial that you practise good hygiene regimes, like using gloves and masks and washing your hands and equipment after use.

A microbe's potential negative aspects are promoted far more in the media, particularly concerning the medical consequences of what exposure to harmful microbes can cause. We need to view the microbial world with a more balanced appreciation of all the incredible good they do. There would be no life on the planet without them. The role they play in healthy living soil is vital if you want to achieve nutrient-rich disease-free abundant produce from your Smart Garden.

As part of the technograrian approach to your Smart Garden, investment in a 400x microscope is a wise move. These microscopes are inexpensive and can connect to your home computer or even a smartphone for viewing. They allow us to see into this incredible 'Invisiverse' and all the mind-boggling creatures that inhabit this world. You can use it on your soil or the compost teas you have created and view the thousands of different bacteria and perhaps a nematode or even a flagellate or amoeba! These are fantastic for seeing the living activity in your soil. As your soil health improves, you will know you are on the right track with these tiny critter populations radically increasing in numbers and size.

Compost tea is the most easily explainable microbial additive for your garden. Suppose you have ever looked at really decomposed compost at the bottom of a compost pile. In that case, you can see it is alive with tiny microscopic activity even with our limited human vision. Most of the activity we can see are much larger lifeforms that are feeding on these microbes. Those, in turn, will become prey for even larger lifeforms. Ultimately, they will become prey for the kings of the compost and soil jungle . . . the worms!

Compost tea in its simplest form requires you to take some of that compost that is the most decomposed and place it in a large bucket of warm water. The microbes contained in the compost will be washed from the compost into the water, and we can then spray this water onto our soil. This allows us to increase the number and spread of microbes over our garden.

While this is effective, many microbes do not survive the process. It will again take time and repeated applications to build our soil microbe numbers. Let's take that same bucket of compost tea and add microbial food in the form of sugars (we use molasses) and aerate it while continually stirring the tea. Those microbial populations will grow far more extensive in number. Now when we apply the new supercharged compost tea to our soil, we will see a far faster response in the way of improved plant health and yields.

Compost tea brewers come in all shapes, sizes and costs and are available through many outlets. You can purchase microbial dry bases and liquids from garden centres. Still, these are just a convenient version of the simple compost tea we previously discussed. If your compost pile is not yet at the necessary decomposition point and ready for use, they can be an option. Some soil amendment products you can purchase will also claim to be 'inoculated'. This means that the manufacturer has sprayed or added microbial populations to the product. Often products like pre-bagged manure and biochar will say that it has been inoculated. I am not sure how effective this is because we do not generally buy these products. Our experience has shown us that microbes tend to be relatively fragile and can be dramatically affected by heat and cold and too little or too much oxygen.

In biodynamic gardening communities, microbial populations found in cow manure and minerals are mixed, placed in cow horns and buried in the ground for some time. The microbial/manure/mineral mix is then tapped out of the horn and applied as supercompost for direct use on garden beds or used to create a compost tea.

Over the years, we have tried many different composting methods and have always had a program of creating compost teas. Sometimes we use not only compost but various plant materials known to have high levels of certain nutrients. We call these 'green teas' as they are often made from green plant material that can be soaked in water, and then that water is sprayed either on the soil or plants themselves. We use a green tea made from willow bark as a germination and growth promoter on young seedlings. Willow bark contains indole-butyric acid, which is a hormone that promotes root growth and is entirely natural. It is also a natural pain reliever!

We are currently burying our kitchen garden waste directly into our garden beds. With our Smart Garden, we are always looking for ways to reduce our workload and the time required to maintain the garden. By burying our kitchen scraps directly into the garden, we create greater diversity in the microbial populations at the various stages of decomposition of the waste.

We are also currently trialling a new 12-week Living Grocery Shop concept in our garden. We produce various vegetables and fruit every week that replicates what we would buy at the local grocery store. Our direct-to-garden composting regime will be a vital part of that new program. It effectively recycles our organic home waste and rebuilds soil health and soil volume in our beds. We see benefits in this 12-week approach to supplying our family requirements as it reduces the need for storage and preservation of over-harvests and, therefore, the potential of wastage.

We are also aware of the possibility of creating an anaerobic environment in our soil. Anaerobic conditions were previously seen as unwanted, but the latest soil research is finding that anaerobic microbial populations also offer gardens some great benefits. So far, our trialling of direct-to-garden kitchen scrap composting is getting great results with a pronounced increase in worm populations and aeration of the soil.

Soil microbiology is a vast topic that could take several books to explore fully. Adding microbes to poor soil will achieve little as they will simply die without an abundance of moist decomposing organic matter, nutrients and minerals in the soil. I have not even touched on the importance of mycorrhizal fungi to garden health, or predatory nematodes, or our beloved kings of the garden, our worms.

I just wanted to highlight some of how a technograrian gardening approach – using the latest research from science – can substantially reduce the work required and radically increase the amount your Smart Garden can produce.

STEP 8: FEEDING AND CARE OF YOUR GARDEN

One of the best ways to improve plant health and yield is by feeding your plants the vital nutrients and minerals they need through their leaves and stems. The actual point of absorption is through the stomata and less so via their epidermis. Stomata are like tiny windows or mouths on leaves that can absorb water and liquids and are used by the plant to exchange gases. Studies have shown that plant absorption rates move through the plant at about 1 foot per hour and nutrients in the liquids applied to the plants reach all areas of the plant. The plants require humidity to absorb the nutrients as aerosols via their stomata.

We use foliar sprays to bridge any shortfall in nutrient availability in the soil and to supply a needed push at specific times in a plant's growth cycle. Foliar sprays that are high in nitrogen (N), potassium (K) and phosphorus (P), and many other trace nutrients, are a way to feed plants these essential requirements directly.[164] When we first built our Smart Garden, our soil was still too 'hot' or 'green' to be fully bioavailable to the plants we were trying to grow. We were adding manures and mineral amendments, but these needed time to decompose to a point where they would be available to our plants. Foliar spraying helped supply the much-needed nutrients the plants required to get started and grow.

Initially, we were spraying the garden every week or so with different liquid fertilisers, and the results were immediate. Over the years, our soils have improved dramatically. We now have a program of soil rebuilding that considers soil decomposition timeframes. We have been able to reduce the amount of foliar spraying we do. We no longer use it to mitigate our soil's inability to supply nutrients to the plants but to supply a nutrient boost at points when the plants need a kick in nutrient levels.

This approach radically increases plant health and, particularly, gross yields. Initially, we would strike seeds in seedling trays and then plant out the seedlings into our beds. In our constant search for ways to reduce the time and effort required in maintaining our garden, we now generally sow directly into our garden beds.

Our *Hügelkultur* bed design also helps increase our soil temperatures for seed germination, as does the protected garden space. As the decomposing wood and material in the bottom of our beds generates heat for the soil, it also buffers cold soil temperatures coming from the ground underneath them. This increase in soil temperature in conjunction with the abundance of moisture and organic matter in the soil makes seed germination relatively easy. We also use our foliar sprays or liquid fertilisers to 'wet in' the seeds, providing the new taproots with a perfect environment from which to sprout.

After we see the seedling develop, we generally leave it until it gets to a point where it will begin to generate its first flush of plant bulk. This is on average between four and eight weeks into its growth cycle. (Obviously, I am generalising my descriptions as plant variety and types will require more specific information but, hopefully, you get the idea.)

We apply another foliar spray that will support this significant growth phase of the plant. Before these growth phases, plants assess the environment in which they find themselves and decide how to express themselves best given the conditions. Hopefully, your plants will find that they have an ideal amount of sunlight, water and food and set their growth profile to maximum abundance! We find this is where a liquid fertiliser can have enormous benefit.

The other stage of the growth cycle that we find foliar sprays can play a critical role in is just before the plant's fruiting or flowering stage. When we see the plant is almost at the point at which it will begin to fruit or flower, we again apply a spray directly to the leaves and stems that is high in NPK and trace elements and minerals. When used on something like a tomato plant, the difference in yields can be quite staggering. This turbocharging hit of nutrients gives the plant the green light to overproduce. We have increased yields by 200 to 300 per cent by using foliar sprays at these critical junctures.

Another excellent use for foliar sprays is if a plant starts to look ill or diseased. Hopefully, your organic Smart Garden is the picture of health, but things can happen that can cause your garden to become sick. We once let a local gardener come into our garden who had not cleaned his equipment correctly. He inadvertently brought a disease in with him.

Garden sanitisation is critically essential, and it was our lesson in understanding the damage that can result if not followed. Now we are super-selective about plants that come in from other gardens. While we can never be 100 per cent certain that a seedling or plant is healthy, any plant that even looks like it could potentially have an issue is not allowed into the garden.

In the case of introduced disease on our tomato plants, we were able to use our foliar sprays to nurse all our plants back to full health. We felt that this was a better course of action than just removing them immediately (which we also do when necessary) because it would help develop resistance in our future plantings from the seeds we would collect at the end of the season.

Many people were shocked that we could bring the plants back to full production health using foliar sprays. It showed us how effective good quality liquid fertilisers could be in disease mitigation.

Foliar sprays can be applied using a simple manual hand-pump spray bottle or a motorised misting sprayer. Both will be available at your local gardening or hardware store. Early-morning spraying is more effective than spraying later in the day, as stomata are open during the morning, when the plant uses them to absorb the morning dew from their leaves. The finer the mist settings on your sprayer, the greater the chance of the plant absorbing the aerosol. This will increase the effectiveness of the foliar spray.

Another tip is not to saturate the plant. Leaves dripping with liquid fertiliser could decrease absorption levels, as stomata will close if too much liquid is present. You also risk burning your plants if the liquid in the foliar spray is too concentrated. It is important to mist the leaves' undersides, as these areas have the greatest stomata concentration.

Foliar spraying is a vital part of our technograrian approach to our Smart Garden. Foliar spraying as a concept has not been around for long when put in the context of our agrarian past. I have had many gardeners, both home-based and commercial, come into our garden and ask for tips and tricks. I give them a jar of the latest foliar spray we are using, and they often look at the bottle with a degree of scepticism. I often find that when I ask them how they went, they usually tell me they have not got around to using it yet. There seems to be resistance from some gardeners as to the validity of foliar sprays. Still, from our experience, they are incredibly crucial in not only making your garden flourish but making your Smart Garden life a lot easier.

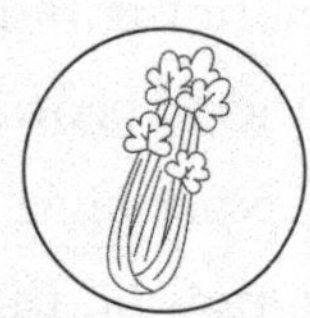

STEP 9: HARVESTING AND STORAGE

The most exciting time for your Smart Garden will be harvest time. We have moved away from harvesting all of a crop at one time and adopted a more grazing type approach through the harvest-able period. When the harvest looks like it is coming to an end and there is a risk that fruit and produce could become spoiled if left any longer, we harvest totally and use the crop to create the supply we will preserve for winter and the nonproductive months.

Initially, we found that eating parts of a plant while growing made some plants falter or become diseased. We had heard many stories from the past of people grazing off a lettuce plant over several weeks by only removing a few leaves every couple of days and waiting for new ones to appear. After a few grazing harvests, our reality was that plants seem to lose vitality and production of fresh leaves slowed or even stopped. This was usually when garden pests like aphids and whitefly would attack the plant, and we would be left with no choice but to remove the plant from the garden.

A garden that could be grazed seemed like an ideal way to feed our family the freshest produce, as harvest could take place moments before we consumed it, maximising our nutritional benefit, so we felt we needed to persevere and find what the issue may have been. Some plants like tomatoes and cucumbers are perfectly designed for this style of garden consumption. But we found these too could become compromised by this approach. We began super-feeding these plants with things like our foliar sprays as we grazed on them and found this increase in available nutrients mitigated many of the problems.

The issue with this is that bathing lettuce in a seaweed emulsion every week became a bit off-putting when it came time to eat it. Vegetables that can be washed easily presented a better proposition at dinner time. Our kids became experts at looking at every aspect of a lettuce leaf to ensure that it did not contain leftover spray residue.

The smell that emanates from your Smart Garden after a good foliar spray can be likened at times to a spoiling bin of fish. Both Gemma and I love the smell because we associate it with a stunning healthy garden. On the other hand, our kids are not quite so convinced, and any possibility of it ending up on a dinner plate is to be avoided at all cost. Luckily, as our soil health improved, the need to spray the plants became less and less. We can now happily graze on all the plants in our garden without using many amendments or sprays. The soil now provides all the vitality they require, and many of our problems have vanished!

We do all the bottling, pickling and preserving of our end-of-season garden harvest. Every year, we make the process faster and more streamlined. Preserving a crop in this way is immensely rewarding, but it does require a reasonable amount of time and patience. What we have been doing more and more every year is blanching and freezing the surplus from harvests, and the results have been delightfully surprising.

This year we applied this method of long-term storage to carrots and eggplants as well. Grabbing these from a freezer for a midwinter meal is an absolute joy. While not as nutritionally beneficial as fresh produce, it allows us to reduce wastage to almost zero. The process is quick and easy, and we store them in meal-sized portions, so we always use the amount in full.

There are many excellent books and lots of information on preserving and food storage methods for your harvested produce, so I will not dive too deeply into it here. As I will discuss in the next chapter, your protected Smart Garden will extend the natural growing season, so your ability to graze from your garden will cover many more weeks and months than a typical garden.

Storage comes down to creativity and waste minimisation. We get creative with pickling recipes, jams and chutneys. Gemma has created a bottled minced garlic recipe that is simply amazing. As with anything to do with our Smart Garden, we are always looking for ways we can minimise input (work) while maximising output (produce) and safely preserving and storing an array of super-yummy things is a wonderful way of maximising!

STEP 10: EXTENDING THE NATURAL CYCLES (TEMPERATURE CONTROL AND WATERING)

Your Smart Garden's ability to extend your region's natural growing season is one of the significant benefits of a protected garden space. In Tasmania, there is an old saying that you 'never plant your tomatoes before Show Day'. Show Day is a reference to the Hobart Agricultural Show, held in mid-October every year. It is the time many people get to show off their garden produce and homemade wares. The warning comes from the region's propensity to have a spring frost that can kill off young tomato plants and seedlings.

Many avid local home gardeners follow this advice and, in turn, can end up with diminished yields if our regional spring/summer season is mild or finishes early. Some take the chance and plant their tomatoes before Show Day and keep their fingers crossed for a frost-free spring. This decision alone can take up a good part of any garden conversation in Tasmania in the lead-up to summer.

With our Smart Garden, we plant our tomatoes in early September, or even August, without any fear of a deadly frost wiping out our crop. We also know that a mild summer will not be an issue inside our protected garden. It will always be hot enough to ripen fruit and extend summer benefits well into autumn. This ability to prolong our growing season massively helps the financial viability of our garden.

We can be producing fresh vegetables and fruits well before and well after other gardens start and finish. This creates more demand for the things you have to sell, trade or barter, as they are not readily available from others when you have them. A Smart Garden will also hold heat for extended periods in the day, bringing plants to harvest in shorter timeframes. This allows us to double-crop certain varieties over a single season. As we are big proponents of stagger planting, it makes the garden's harvested volume potential quite prolific. It shows how we can produce hundreds of kilos of tomatoes in a relatively small area.

As the garden has also been harvesting its rainwater over the winter, we have collected enough to supply ample water to the garden in the warmer months. This not only keeps our garden bed soil lovely and moist, but it will also generate enough humidity to make sure the plants are not stressed during the summer.

At the peak of summer, we also run a misting system from the ceiling that stops the layering of too much hot air and creates a cooling downdraft. As we are using an automated irrigation drip system, no drop of water goes to waste. What is not immediately absorbed by the soil also goes into creating humidity in the garden.

A vegetable garden loves around 50 per cent relative humidity. With the harvested water and automated systems, we can easily achieve this all year round.

We have hygrometers that measure heat and humidity throughout the garden. They report information to the main screen in our kitchen. If heat is starting to build and humidity is dropping, we are alerted, and we can go and open more heat vents and manually turn on more misting systems. Plants become susceptible to stress after about 28 degrees Celsius. Though they can handle short periods of warmer weather, we generally like to keep ambient temperatures below 36 degrees Celsius maximum.

This is one of the main benefits of a protected ventilated garden over a traditional greenhouse, particularly in locations with scorching summer temperatures. The capability to move heated air out of your garden and have it replaced by cooler air is critical. Having an automated system of solar-powered extraction fans makes life in and for your garden extremely easy. We find that there is generally little wind on sweltering days to help move air in and around your garden. While we have fans placed strategically around the garden, the solar-powered roof-mounted extraction fans act like an emergency heat-purging system.

While temperatures in Tasmania are mild compared to much of the world, we can still have hot days and high summer heats. The one aspect of climate change we can rely on is the weather's ability to keep setting records for the hottest days.

Having our garden within an environment that can alleviate these extreme variances is vital to managing our family's food supply successfully. As the structure stops snow falling on our garden beds in winter, so does it allow us to cool the air with heat extraction and misting systems in summer. This means that we have a growing season that can effectively start in late winter and extend to late autumn. This enormously increases the volume of food we can produce by weeks and months. This ability takes a Smart Garden from being just a garden to what we believe is a food production system for the future.

At our farm, we have winds in September that can play havoc with young seedlings. For many years when our garden was outside and unprotected, we would watch the strong winds push the seedlings almost to the ground, often over several hours and even days. This amount of wind dramatically affects plant growth, and research has shown that it can reduce yields by up to 70 per cent.

Without our protected Smart Garden space, we would be faced with the decision to delay planting until after the winds had subsided and then potentially not have enough time through summer for plants to grow and ripen fully. This would mean accepting lower yields, needing a more extensive garden area and planting even more seedlings.

This is just another example of how having a protected garden space dramatically reduces the effort and work required in your garden and maximises the potential harvests and yields. We have lived through many years of having days and weeks of work lost in a single weather event that may have lasted only a few hours. Whether it be rain, wind, too much heat or a nightly raid by a bunch of marauding animals, these things can destroy your motivation to continue with your garden. Being able to control these aspects of the weather, even to some degree, means you are almost assured that your work will reap the rewards. At the same time, there are always minor issues you still need to navigate. A protected garden space allows you to rely on its output, year after year, with a much higher degree of certainty.

Gemma and I recently spent a day at a beautiful garden farm not far from us. It was the culmination of more than 20 years of work by an avid gardener and self-sufficiency stalwart. As we toured her garden and saw the fantastic work that had been done and systems that were in place, we were nothing but impressed. The family had lived from the garden for years. It was a perfect model of on-farm recycling with manures from the animals used for mulches and compost that produced green fodder crops for the animals.

During our conversations over a cup of tea later in the day, the garden's proud owner lamented that the only thing she wished she had done was to have it all in a protected space. She noted that the many hours of weekly work required to maintain such a garden needed to be driven by both a passion and the necessity to supply food for their family. They lived remotely, and a quick trip to the store was not an option for them, so the garden had to become their supermarket.

As Gemma and I discussed their incredible garden later in the day, we were thankful that we had decided to bite the bullet and build our protected garden space all those years ago. It was driven by our frustration at seeing our hard work destroyed by weather events or unwanted guests and the need to have a reliable food supply for our family.

Our dream was to have a self-sufficient garden that we could be totally reliant on year after year. We knew that while traditional gardens have historically met the needs of millions of people worldwide, the times have changed. Weather events have become more extreme over recent years. They have dramatically impacted a traditional garden's reliability to provide the surety that many people need.

Your Smart Garden will allow you to ensure that, whatever weather and environmental issues you face, you will be able to create a food production system that is much more reliable than a traditional garden. By being able to extend growing seasons in your location using technology and automation, ensuring your crops are not destroyed by extreme weather events and providing an environment in which plants can unconditionally flourish, your Smart Garden can provide a year-round food supply with a minimum of effort.

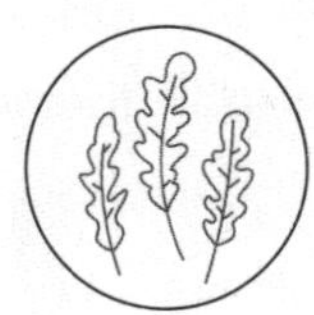

STEP 11: SECURING YOUR GARDEN

I hope that humanity will find a way to navigate and find the solutions for all the problems and issues we face now and will face in the future. If things do become more dire, your protected Smart Garden offers a higher security level than a traditional garden, even for a short period. Suppose, unfortunately, we are faced with a situation where the availability of basic foodstuffs does become compromised. In that case, we will all confront the panic that hunger creates.

How you manage your Smart Garden's production output in those times will be up to you. Being able to provide for your family as well as friends and community will be enormously empowering. The issue will be that desperation can cause even the most usually calm and rational people to behave differently. If it became a situation in which, for the benefit of the greatest number of people, you needed to ration your garden's production, you want to be in a position where you are making those decisions.

If others raid your garden and you lose your food, then all the effort and vision you have shown in creating your Smart Garden will be for nothing.

There is a limit to how much you can secure your garden. What a Smart Garden does offer is an ability to reduce the potential of becoming a victim of a crime of opportunity. Having a garden out in the open will undoubtedly increase your chances of having your produce stolen. We often see this, unfortunately, occur in open community gardens. Usually, the theft of produce is only half of the issue. Destruction of the garden by intruders, as they tear through it, is of equal concern. A Smart Garden at least gives you the ability to monitor and protect an enclosed space. Placing locks on doors and reducing the ability to access the garden will be relatively easy.

We use solar-powered sensor lights in our garden. These have been invaluable for alerting us that we may have left a door open and are now being visited by local wildlife. Installing CCTV cameras could also be an option. During our time in the hemp industry, we have seen protected cropping spaces used to grow medicinal-grade hemp plants that have been incredibly secure due to government regulation.

These needed to include security measures like high electrified fences and swipe cards for entry into the gardens. These facilities showed us how secure a Smart Garden could potentially be. Still, I believe that if your garden required this level of security, you may have other issues that would be more troubling than protecting your carrots!

If you are faced with many people who really want the produce from your garden, there will not be much you can do to stop them.

A protected Smart Garden is inherently more secure than other options, should these problems present themselves. We hope and pray that we never find ourselves in the circumstances where we need to protect our food supply from others. It is, though, a situation that many people all over the world face every day. It would be naive to think that it could never happen to us, and the creation of your protected Smart Garden is at least some form of acknowledgement of that.

STEP 12: TIME TO ENJOY!

While in no way exhaustive or overly prescriptive, the preceding chapters give you an outline of how to construct, design and manage your Smart Garden. Each chapter represents a departure point for your own research and ideas. As I have expounded in this book, protected cropping, soil microbiology, organic foliar supplementation, irrigation and automation, and the many other areas incorporated into Smart Garden design and management are exploding with research and updated information.

I appreciate that people love an exhaustive how-to in their areas of interest. Still, with the rapid growth of new and exciting information in this area, I felt it better to give you an outline of the ideas and concepts that could frame a departure point for your personal Smart Garden journey. By the very act of writing this book, I know that somewhere in my future, someone is going to show me their Smart Garden. It is going to be something far beyond what even I can imagine now. Maybe it will be an incredible home garden; maybe it will be part of a community collective or even a local council initiative. Perhaps it could even be feeding a new human colony on Mars!

Getting your protected structure designed and built and your garden beds full of wholesome soil is the first and most crucial step. It represents the largest single area of cost and the most amount of physical work. Once you are at this stage, though, you can begin planting and seeing the real fruits of your labour. As we are continually learning more and implementing new things with our garden, it would be a disservice to promote the idea that a Smart Garden is a final destination. As is central to the technograrian approach, the inclusion of the latest science and technology means that your garden will constantly evolve, just like electric cars and solar power.

To me, that represents the fascinating aspect of a Smart Garden. Having something as historically fundamental to all of us as growing food but incorporating new knowledge and understanding is eminently exciting and rewarding. While your garden will deliver on all the health, environmental, financial and insurance benefits I have outlined, it will still not have achieved its true value or potential. That will be for tomorrow. Who knows if millions of people worldwide will take up the challenge of personal responsibility and become more food secure? I hope that many people will do so and that this collective power will be instrumental in driving profound change in the world.

As we join together in this vision of a better tomorrow and create and develop our Smart Gardens, we will all share in the bounty it gives us. The most remarkable benefit will not just be the incredible food it produces, the environmental advantages or the security it gives us. It will be the hope for a better future and the time to enjoy it.

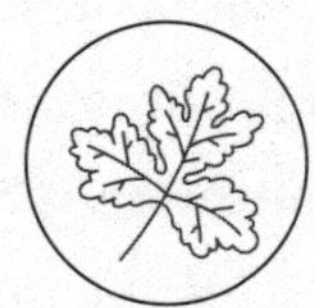

OUR FOOD FUTURE

'The greatest change we need to make is from consumption to production, even if on a small scale, in our own gardens. If only 10% of us do this, there is enough for everyone. Hence the futility of revolutionaries who have no gardens, who depend on the very system they attack, and who produce words and bullets, not food and shelter.'

– Bill Mollison

We can all probably agree that we are in a period of tremendous and profound change. Much of that change will be thrust upon us by forces beyond our control. Those forces will have many forms, be they political, economic or technological. As part of this period, though, we will still get to determine how much we let happen to us and how much we control ourselves, even in small ways.

I would like to think that this book will motivate you to consider creating your own Smart Garden. If I look introspectively at what exactly motivated Gemma and me to create ours, I believe at its core was the need to regain our self-determination. In the last 50 years, it is one area of all our lives that has been eroded to the point of relative extinction.

While no one would argue that we all want to be the masters of our destiny, the fact is, we have all surrendered our liberty and, therefore, responsibility in the pursuit of security. We personally learned that security was not guaranteed during the Black Saturday bushfire more than ten years ago, and more recently with the COVID-19 pandemic. These events can easily be much bigger than the institutions we have set up to save us from them.

Part of regaining the ability to self-determine our own lives is knowing that the things that are critical to our health and happiness are back in our control. The responsibility aspect comes from knowing you have provided real food security to yourself and your family. It is also accepting the responsibility that we are all playing our role in destroying the Earth and contributing to other people's suffering on the planet. Every trip to a supermarket destroys more forest, erodes more soil, contaminates more ocean and covers some faraway country with plastic waste. It is not someone else's trolley. It is the one you and I pushed around this week. The number of items we place in the trolley only exacerbates the damage that is caused. A Smart Garden will mean less in that trolley. Less, not more, is what the world needs now in every way.

Let's look at a Smart Garden as being a key to regaining our self-determination. It is interesting to overview the three factors that psychologists believe are needed to motivate us to be more self-determined. These are autonomy, competence and connectedness:

Autonomy is defined as knowing that our direct personal actions make a difference or change for the better.

Competence is feeling like we are learning and becoming masters of a new skillset or process that has value.

Connectedness is experiencing a sense of belonging or attachment to other people.

Your Smart Garden will give you autonomy in knowing that your small backyard garden is making a real difference to the health of yourself, your family and the world at large. It will also empower you with a sense of competence as you learn and master growing organic, nutritious food you will delight in and share. Connectedness will come from knowing that you are now united with the multitude of other people who are making real-world changes for a better future. Connectedness might simply manifest in creating the opportunity for you to pass some of your produce over a fence to a neighbour. That could start a conversation that begins a friendship. Do that several different times, and who knows, you might begin to build your community!

Perhaps the motivation you need to start your Smart Garden is something different. While no one can reliably predict what the future of food is, you have a choice to let corporations determine it for you and accept the unknown ramifications of that decision. Or you can determine your own food future and remove the reliance on a system that is neither healthy, sustainable or secure.

I see and read many news articles and reports on how we need to change how we produce and consume food urgently. The industrialised practices of large-scale food manufacture are coming under continual scrutiny. The chorus of economic and environmental leaders who see the need for urgent action is growing louder and louder. I am boosted by the fact that corporate financial power is no longer silencing dissent. The main alternative presented is a return to small organic farms supplying the needs of local communities.

While this is obviously a great idea and is already happening with progressive communities, I fear that once profit becomes the driving motive or demand outstrips supply, a financial opportunity will be recognised. When these things happen, the same corporate contrivances always come into play. Do we want Big Ag to become Big Organic? How will we know and trust that the change is real? We already see the 'greenwashing' of companies and corporations with little or no proper mandate for sustainable change. Their sole focus is on investment return and growth. Is that not precisely what got us here in the first place?

Can we not take that extra step that sees localised also become micro-localised? Any aerial image of typical suburban backyards will see hundreds of swimming pools taking pride of place within them. Those same backyards could also contain their own Smart Garden for a fraction of the cost of those swimming pools. Suppose all those families were eating homegrown healthy fresh produce as part of their diets. Would that not positively impact the population's health? Suppose those families were reducing their environmental impact by 20, 30 or 50 per cent. Would that reduction, when multiplied by hundreds, if not thousands, of families not directly impact the environment and climate change?

We need to be closer to our food. For me, a future food system with infinite merit would be a combination of local organic small-scale food producers and home-based Smart Gardens. The local organic farm that supplies variety and diversity to what our Smart Gardens can produce becomes an essential part of a truly healthy diet. However, this approach eliminates the need for them to produce a hundred lettuces a week and then a thousand. We know how that story goes.

Could it be that in the future of solar-powered planes, electric-powered cars and our planet's re-greening, future home design will also include Smart Gardens within them? Would governments be willing to incentivise that change financially? Once, we were fascinated to see solar panels on a home. They represented the possibility of a healthier, cleaner and more sustainable future. I know a Smart Garden represents that same possibility. All it will take is for someone to see a friend or neighbour serving fresh homegrown organic food to their family for the change to begin. I will be fascinated to see who the first people are that take up the challenge of creating a Smart Garden for themselves.

I did not want to overwhelm the readers of this book by diving too deeply into every possible iteration and aspect of a Smart Garden. There is enough for the self-starters to begin their Smart Garden journey, and we offer those needing direct help and information more support via our website at www.thesmartveggiepatch.com.

Our garden is the living centre of our home and family. We did not plan for it to be, that is just how it has evolved. A lush garden, an oasis, a place that nourishes every part of who we are. The lush garden is central to our human history and our earliest stories and mythologies. It draws us to it from a place deep within ourselves. As we have destroyed many of the places that naturally occurred around the world, could it be that we can each rebuild a part of it? Being so profoundly involved with our garden's living cycle has given us far greater appreciation and respect for that same living cycle in nature.

I actually just took a break from writing this closing chapter to make Gemma and myself some lunch. As I pondered what to put on our pita bread wraps, I walked to our garden and grabbed some mixed lettuce leaves, parsley, baby spinach, cucumber, radishes and a tomato. While my mind was partly lost in the heady creative pursuit of writing, I realised what I had just done. For the sake of a somewhat homely but authentic example of Smart Garden living,

I retraced and counted the steps of my previous journey. It took just 48 steps (and a sharp knife) to harvest the freshest possible bounty of organic salad items for our lunch. Within literally seconds from harvest and while still at its optimum peak of nutritional value, my body consumed the same produce. No carbon footprint, no plastic, no chemicals, no soil erosion and not one forest was cut down. Just 48 steps for us to create the very healthiest lunch that is humanly possible!

I love the fact that when my children discuss their dreams for their own homes, it always includes their own gardens. They see it as a normal part of family life, a necessity like a bedroom or a bathroom. Even as the eldest ones leave home to venture out into the world, a home visit is never complete until they have a box of fresh produce tucked under their arm. As a role model for future generations, this normalisation of self-sufficient, sustainable and responsible living is undoubtedly a step in the right direction.

I hope this book inspires you to start your Smart Garden right now. Your health, the environment and your future food security will be the benefactors of your vision and enterprise. It just takes that tiny spark of inspiration that comes from the belief in a better tomorrow. I like to imagine that sometime soon, as the relentless news cycle promotes the latest environmental crisis, war, famine or economic collapse, a child with wide eyes will ask a parent about what the future will look like. That parent will smile and take the child by the hand and walk them into a lush, abundant Smart Garden, and in there, the child will see all they need to know and understand.

ACKNOWLEDGEMENTS

I would like to thank the following people who presented like the stars they are in the universal alignment that made this book possible.

(In order of celestial appearance) Gemma Lynch-Memory, my ever-present co-conspirator in all things crazy. From six children to Smart Gardens, hemp companies, art galleries and now a book! All approached with the same sense of giddy enthusiasm. Motto: Hold hands and jump! Natasha Wilde, editor extraordinaire and my longtime suspicious fact-checker. Tara Wynne from Curtis Brown for your vision and gracious addition of stardust superpower. Ingrid Ohlsson from Pan Macmillan, for taking my expectations and exceeding them by a billion. Brianne Collins from Pan Macmillan for all of your help and support in making it real.

For Pop, who first took me by the hand and led me into his garden and showed me all that I ever needed to know.

W.E. Poole – 1925–2022

ENDNOTES

1 Chris Otter, 'Feast and Famine: The Global Food Crisis', 2010, Origins.osu.edu. Available at: https://origins.osu.edu/article/feast-and-famine-global-food-crisis?language_content_entity=en

2 Centre for International Governance Innovation., Clapp, J. and Cohen, M., 2009. *Global Food Crisis: Governance Challenges and Opportunities (Studies in international governance series)*. Wilfrid Laurier University Press

3 Food and Agriculture Organization of the United Nations (FAO), 2014. *Food Wastage Footprint: Full Cost Accounting – Final Report.* [online] FAO. Available at: http://www.fao.org/3/i3991e/i3991e.pdf

4 Nhlbi.nih.gov. 2021. *Americans poor diet drives $50 billion a year in health care costs.* [online] Available at: https://www.nhlbi.nih.gov/news/2019/americans-poor-diet-drives-50-billion-year-health-care-costs

5 I wanted to find a word that best encapsulated the merging of technology with traditional gardening. Technograrian came to me one night as I was dozing off to sleep and I felt quite clever to have come up with it. Further research the next morning, though, proved my moment of creative serendipity was perhaps not as original as I had thought. The word was apparently first used in a 2010 draft strategic plan from the National Restoration Party of Zambia on ways to build their 'Green Economy'. No reference is made to who actually came up with the word but having already been to the beautiful country that is Zambia, I look forward to perhaps one day returning and further investigating who that initial clever wordsmith might be!

6 Strauss, W., & Howe, N. *The Fourth Turning: an American Prophecy*, Broadway Books, New York, 1997

7 'How many people die of hunger each year?', The World Counts, 20/06/2020, https://www.theworldcounts.com/challenges/people-and-poverty/hunger-and-obesity/how-many-people-die-from-hunger-each-year

8 'Food Security', Lexico.com, 20/06/2020, https://www.lexico.com/definition/food_security

9 'Just in Time (JIT)', Investopedia, 21/06/2020, https://www.investopedia.com/terms/j/jit.asp

10 Jean Anthelme Brillat-Savarin, 2011. *The Physiology of Taste*. [online] Barnes & Noble. Available at: https://www.barnesandnoble.com/w/physiology-of-taste-jean-anthelme-brillat-savarin/1100255367

11 *Anthropological materialism of Feuerbach on the essence of man and religion*. [online] Tostpost.com. Available at: https://tostpost.com/news-and-society/21603-anthropological-materialism-of-feuerbach-on-the-essence-of-man-and-rel.html

12 Lindlahr, V., 1991. *You Are What You Eat*. San Bernardino, Calif.: Borgo Press.

13 Australian Competition and Consumer Commission. 2021. *Federal Court finds Coles' 'Freshly Baked' and 'Baked Today' marketing claims misleading*. [online] Available at: https://www.accc.gov.au/media-release/federal-court-finds-coles%E2%80%99-%E2%80%98freshly-baked%E2%80%99-and-%E2%80%98baked-today%E2%80%99-marketing-claims-misleading

14 Agrilinks. 2021. *Food Quality and Safety in the Global Food Security Index*. [online] Available at: https://www.agrilinks.org/post/food-quality-and-safety-global-food-security-index-0

15 Transportenvironment.org. 2021. *Shipping and climate change* [online] Available at: https://www.transportenvironment.org/what-we-do/shipping-and-environment/shipping-and-climate-change

16 Farah, Troy, 'Banned Bread', *The Guardian*, 2019, https://www.theguardian.com/us-news/2019/may/28/bread-additives-chemicals-us-toxic-america

17 Dunphy, S. and Dunphy, V., 2021. 'Majority of the world's population depends on imported food'. [online] *European Scientist*. Available at: https://www.europeanscientist.com/en/agriculture/majority-of-the-worlds-population-depends-on-imported-food/

18 Gustafson, S., 'Global Report on Food Crises: 135 million in 55 countries faced acute hunger in 2019'. 2021. [online] Available at: https://www.ifpri.org/blog/global-report-food-crises-135-million-55-countries-faced-acute-hunger-2019

19 Dan Flynn, 'Imports and Exports: Americans Shop the World for Food Every Day of the Week', Food Safety News, 2013, https://www.foodsafetynews.com/2013/11/americans-dining-on-more-imported-food-than-ever/

20 Rich Weismann, 'Today's supply chains are too lean', Supply Chain Drive, 2020, https://www.supplychaindive.com/news/lean-supply-chain-jit-inventory-covid-19/574693/

21 Wharton Online. 2021. *Business Impacts of COVID-19 (and How They'll Affect the Future)*. [online] Available at: https://online.wharton.upenn.edu/blog/how-coronavirus-will-affect-the-future/

22 Eric Holt-Giménez and Loren Peabody, 'From Food Rebellions to Food Sovereignty: Urgent call to fix a broken food system', Institute for Food and Development Policy, May 16, 2008

23 Lowyinstitute.org. 2021. 'Crew-change crisis risks supply chains – and lives'. [online] Available at: https://www.lowyinstitute.org/the-interpreter/crew-shift-crisis-risks-supply-chains-and-lives

24 FAO Report, 'The impact of natural hazards and disasters on agriculture and food security and nutrition', Food and Agriculture Organization, 2015, http://www.fao.org/3/a-i4434e.pdf

25 FAO Report, 'The impact of natural hazards and disasters on agriculture and food security and nutrition', Food and Agriculture Organization, 2015, http://www.fao.org/3/a-i4434e.pdf

26 The Balance. 2021. *Natural Disasters Are a Bigger Threat Than Terrorism.* [online] Available at: https://www.thebalance.com/cost-of-natural-disasters-3306214

27 Oecd.org. 2021. *Global Science Forum reports*. [online] Available at https://www.oecd.org/sti/inno/globalscienceforumreports.htm [Accessed 2 May 2021]

28 Tempag.net. 2021. *Temperate Agriculture*. [online] Available at: https://tempag.net/temperate-agriculture/

29 Maryam Rezaei and Bin Lui, 'Food loss and wastage in the food supply chain', FAO United Nations, July 2017, http://www.fao.org/3/a-bt300e.pdf

30 Dana Gunders, 'Wasted', Natural Resources Defense Council, August 2017, https://www.nrdc.org/resources/wasted-how-america-losing-40-percent-its-food-farm-fork-landfill

31 Department of Agriculture, Water and the Environment. 2021. [online] Available at: https://www.environment.gov.au/protection/waste/food-waste

32 Hannah Ritchie and Max Roser, 'Environmental impacts of food production', Our World in Data, January 2020, https://ourworldindata.org/environmental-impacts-of-food

33 Dana Gunders, 'Wasted', August 2017. Natural Resources Defense Council, https://www.nrdc.org/resources/wasted-how-america-losing-40-percent-its-food-farm-fork-landfill

34 David A. Rasko, 'Outbreak of Shiga Toxin-Producing Escherichia coli (STEC) O157:H7 Associated with Romaine Lettuce Consumption', US National Library of Medicine National Institutes of Health, 2011, https://www.ncbi.nlm.nih.gov/pmc/articles/PMC3563629/

35 World Bank. 2021. *Food-borne Illnesses Cost US$ 110 Billion Per Year in Low- and Middle-Income Countries*. [online] Available at: https://www.worldbank.org/en/news/press-release/2018/10/23/food-borne-illnesses-cost-us-110-billion-per-year-in-low-and-middle-income-countries

36 Who.int. 2021. *Food safety*. [online] Available at: https://www.who.int/news-room/fact-sheets/detail/food-safety

37 Ritchie, H. and Roser, M., 2021. *Causes of Death*. [online] Our World in Data. Available at: https://ourworldindata.org/causes-of-death

38 Who.int. 2021. [online] Available at: https://www.who.int/influenza/Global_Influenza_Strategy_2019_2030_Summary_English.pdf?ua=1

39 U.S. Food and Drug Administration. 2021. *FDA 2019 Report on Antimicrobial Sales for Food-Producing Animals*. [online] Available at: https://www.fda.gov/animal-veterinary/cvm-updates/fda-releases-annual-summary-report-antimicrobials-sold-or-distributed-2019-use-food-producing

40 Organ meats: Benefits and risks. (2022). Retrieved 9 March 2022, from https://www.medicalnewstoday.com/articles/319229

41 Emmanuel Bonnard, 'Plastic Pollution is a Global Challenge', Trendsformative, 2020, https://trendsformative.com/plastic-pollution-is-a-global-challenge/

42 Julie Cohen, 'How do we break our addiction to plastic?', University of California – Carbon Neutral Initiative, December 2017, https://www.universityofcalifornia.edu/news/83-billion-metric-tons-plastic-and-counting

43 Joe Curtin, 'Ireland can lead charge in war against plastic', *Irish Times*, January 2018, https://www.irishtimes.com/opinion/ireland-can-lead-charge-in-war-against-plastic-1.3374066

44 'The problem with plastic', 2021. [online] Available at: https://www.take3.org/the-plastic-facts/

45 Mitte. 2021. *The truth about recycling plastic*. [online] Available at: https://mitte.co/2018/07/18/truth-recycling-plastic/

46 Leslie Young, 'Here's how much plastic you might be eating every day', *Global News*, 2019, https://globalnews.ca/news/5352302/microplastic-consumption-health/#:~:text=The%20average%20American%20adult%20consumes,from%20the%20University%20of%20Victoria.

47 Oceana. 2021. *Campaign*. [online] Available at: https://oceana.org/our-campaigns/plastics#:~:text=The%20oceans%20face%20a%20massive,into%20the%20oceans%20every%20minute

48 Thalif Deen, 'Food waste enough to feed the hungry four times over', Reliefweb, 2018, https://reliefweb.int/report/world/food-waste-enough-feed-world-s-hungry-four-times-over

49 Cassidy, West, Gerber & Foley, 'Redefining agricultural yields: from tonnes to people nourished per hectare', *IOP Science*, 2013, https://iopscience.iop.org/article/10.1088/1748–9326/8/3/034015#:~:text=More%20than%20half%20of%20crop,plant%20protein%20(table%202)

50 Douglas Broom, 'South Korea once recycled 2% of its food waste. Now it recycles 95%', World Economic Forum, 2019, https://www.weforum.org/agenda/2019/04/south-korea-recycling-food-waste/#:~:text=As%20far%20back%20as%202005,recycling%20using%20special%20biodegradable%20bags.&text=The%20government%20has%20approved%20the,waste%20recycling%20machines%20in%20Seoul.

51 Joy C. Rickman, Diane M. Barrett and Christine M. Bruhn, 'Nutritional comparison of fresh, frozen and canned fruits and vegetables. Part 1. Vitamins C and B and phenolic compounds', *Journal of the Science of Food and Agriculture*, 2007, https://ucanr.edu/sites/kingscounty/files/19187.pdf

52 Managa, M., Tinyani, P., Senyolo, G., Soundy, P., Sultanbawa, Y. and Sivakumar, D., 2021. 'Impact of transportation, storage, and retail shelf conditions on lettuce quality and phytonutrients losses in the supply chain', *Food, Science and Nutrition*, July 2018, https://onlinelibrary.wiley.com/doi/10.1002/fsn3.685

53 Ibid.

54 Ibid.

55 Scheer & Moss, 2011. 'Dirt poor: Have fruits and vegetables become less nutritious?' [online] *Scientific American*. Available at: https://www.scientificamerican.com/article/soil-depletion-and-nutrition-loss/

56 Ibid.

57 Who.int. 2016. *Anaemia*. [online] Available at: https://www.who.int/health-topics/anaemia#tab=tab_1

58 Marles, R., 2017. 'Mineral nutrient composition of vegetables, fruits and grains: The context of reports of apparent historical declines'. *Journal of Food Composition and Analysis*, Vol. 56, March, pp 93–103

59 Madau, 'Influence of postharvest storage temperature and duration on quality of baby spinach', *American Society for Horticultural Sciences*, 2015, https://journals.ashs.org/horttech/view/journals/horttech/25/5/article-p665.xml

60 Ibid.

61 Gerald Steiner, Bernhard Geissler, Eva S. Schernhammer 'Hunger and obesity as symptoms of non-sustainable food systems and malnutrition', Department of Epidemiology, Center of Public Health, Medical University of Vienna, 2019, https://www.mdpi.com/2076–3417/9/6/1062

62 *Lancet* Commison Report, 'The global syndemic of obesity, undernutrition, and climate change', 2019, https://www.thelancet.com/journals/lancet/article/PIIS0140–6736(18)32822–8/fulltext#seccestitle10

63 Who.int. 2021. *Malnutrition*. [online] Available at: https://www.who.int/news-room/q-a-detail/malnutrition

64 Who.int. 2021. *Obesity*. [online] Available at: https://www.who.int/news-room/facts-in-pictures/detail/6-facts-on-obesity

65 Physicians Committee for Responsible Medicine. 2021. *Diet-Related Diseases Are Leading Cause of Death in U.S.*. [online] Available at: https://

www.pcrm.org/news/health-nutrition/diet-related-diseases-are-leading-cause-death-us

66 Respectful Living. 2021. *41% of US land is used for livestock production according to this report.* [online] Available at: https://www.arespectfullife.com/2018/08/05/41-of-u-s-land-is-used-for-livestock-production/

67 Ibid.

68 Kamangar, F. & Emadi, A., 2021. *Vitamin and mineral supplements: do we really need them?* [online] PubMed. Available at: https://pubmed.ncbi.nlm.nih.gov/22448315/

69 Harvard Health, 2021. *Nutrition's dynamic duos.* [online] Available at: https://www.health.harvard.edu/newsletter_article/Nutritions-dynamic-duos

70 Respectful Living. 2021. *41% of US land is used for livestock production according to this report.* [online] Available at: https://www.arespectfullife.com/2018/08/05/41-of-u-s-land-is-used-for-livestock-production/

71 Ibid.

72 Food and Agriculture Organization of the United Nations. 2021. *News detail.* [online] Available at: http://www.fao.org/soils-2015/news/news-detail/en/c/277682/

73 Chris Arsenault, 2014. 'Only 60 years of farming left if soil degradation continues', [online] *Scientific American.* Available at: https://www.scientificamerican.com/article/only-60-years-of-farming-left-if-soil-degradation-continues/

74 Data.worldbank.org. 2021. *Indicators.* [online] Available at: https://data.worldbank.org/indicator

75 Pimentel and Burgess, 'Soil erosion threatens food production', College of Agriculture and Life Sciences, Cornell University, August 2013, http://www.vetiver.org/USA_pimentel_agriculture-03–00443.pdf

76 The Conversation. 2021. 'Elevated lead levels in Sydney backyards: here's what you can do'. [online] Available at: https://theconversation.com/elevated-lead-levels-in-sydney-back-yards-heres-what-you-can-do-68499

77 Kevin Sheehan, Khristina Narizhnaya and Natalie O'Neill, 2021. *New York Post.* 'High levels of lead in soil poses threat to city gardens'. [online] Available at: https://nypost.com/2019/11/03/high-levels-of-lead-in-soil-poses-threat-to-city-gardens/ [Accessed 24 April 2021].

78 Cat, L., 21 May, 2019. 'Soil erosion washes away $8 billion annually'. [online] *Forbes*. Available at: https://www.forbes.com/sites/linhanhcat/2019/05/21/soil-erosion-washes-away-8-billion/?sh=594fb1c45b6c

79 Accumulation of sodium

80 Intergovernmental Technical Panel on Soils (ITPS), 'Status of the world's soil resources', Food and Agriculture Organizations of the United Nations, 2015, http://www.fao.org/3/i5199e/i5199e.pdf

81 Food and Agriculture Organization, 2015. *Status of the World's Soil Resources: Main Report*. [online] Rome, Italy: FAO. Available at: http://www.fao.org/3/i5199e/i5199e.pdf

82 Chris Arsenault, 2014. 'Only 60 years of farming left if soil degradation continues', [online] *Scientific American*. Available at: https://www.scientificamerican.com/article/only-60-years-of-farming-left-if-soil-degradation-continues/

83 Forum, W., 2021. 'What if the world's soil runs out?'. [online] *TIME*.com. Available at: https://world.time.com/2012/12/14/what-if-the-worlds-soil-runs-out/

84 Odey, Simon & Ogbeche, 'Overview of engineering problems of soil compaction and their effects on growth and yields of crops', 2018, https://www.researchgate.net/publication/328416469_Overview_of_Engineering_Problems_of_Soil_Compaction_and_Their_Effects_on_Growth_and_Yields_of_Crops

85 Fao.org. 2021. [online] Available at: http://www.fao.org/3/i6473e/i6473e.pdf

86 Christopher Johns, 'Living soil, the role of microorganisms in soil health', Northern Australia Land Care Research, 2017, http://www.futuredirections.org.au/publication/living-soils-role-microorganisms-soil-health/

87 Unccd.int. (2010). *United Nations Convention to Combat Desertification*. [online] Available at: https://www.unccd.int/

88 Christina Nunez, 'Desertification explained', *National Geographic*, 2019, https://www.nationalgeographic.com/environment/habitats/desertification/

89 Daniel Cressey, 'Widely used herbicide linked to cancer', *Scientific American*, March 25 2015, https://www.scientificamerican.com/article/widely-used-herbicide-linked-to-cancer/

90 Charles Benbrook, 'Trends in glyphosate herbicide use in the United States and globally', *Environmental Sciences Europe*, February 2016, https://www.ncbi.nlm.nih.gov/pmc/articles/PMC5044953/

91 'What are Organophosphates', Center for Disease Control and Prevention, 2020, https://www.cdc.gov/nceh/clusters/fallon/organophosfaq.htm

92 Damalas and Eleftherohorinos, 'Pesticide exposure, safety issues, and risk assessment indicators', Dept of Environmental Research and Public Health, May 2011, https://www.ncbi.nlm.nih.gov/pmc/articles/PMC3108117/

93 Jess Davis, News Report, ABC News, 2019, https://www.abc.net.au/news/rural/2019–05–14/monsanto-loses-third-verdict-over-weedkiller-roundup/11111034

94 Charles Benbrook, 'Trends in glyphosate herbicide use in the United States and globally', *Environmental Sciences Europe*, 2016, https://www.ncbi.nlm.nih.gov/pmc/articles/PMC5044953/

95 Sue Lanin, 'Organic food: Producers claiming food organic despite not meeting standards', ABC News, October 2016, https://www.abc.net.au/news/2016–10–13/producers-greenwashing-food-to-claim-it-is-organic-choice-says/7930532

96 Dr Edward Group, 'The health dangers of chlorine', *Global Healing*, July 2017, https://globalhealing.com/natural-health/toxic-chemical-health-dangers-chlorine/

97 Markets, R., 2021. *The Worldwide Agrochemicals Industry is Expected to Reach $246.1 Billion by 2025 at a CAGR of 3.4% from 2020.* [online] GlobeNewswire News Room. Available at: https://www.globenewswire.com/news-release/2021/03/24/2198459/28124/en/The-Worldwide-Agrochemicals-Industry-is-Expected-to-Reach-246–1-Billion-by-2025-at-a-CAGR-of-3–4-from-2020.html

98 2021. *Soil Fertility and Erosion.* [online] Available at: https://www.globalagriculture.org/report-topics/soil-fertility-and-erosion.html.

99 Fao.org. 2021. [online] Available at: http://www.fao.org/3/ca6746en/ca6746en.pdf

100 Lu Zhang, Chengxi Yan, Qing Guo, Junbiao Zhang, Jorge Ruiz-Menjivar, 'The impact of agricultural chemical inputs on environment: global evidence from informetrics analysis and visualization', *International Journal of Low-Carbon Technologies*, Volume 13, Issue 4, December 2018, Pages 338–352, https://doi.org/10.1093/ijlct/cty039

101 Ibid.

102 Jenny Howard, 2019. 'Dead zones, explained'. [online] *National Geographic*. Available at: https://www.nationalgeographic.com/environment/article/dead-zones

103 Ibid.

104 Poison.org. 2021. *The Poison Posts*. [online] Available at: https://www.poison.org/the-poison-post

105 Ward MH, Jones RR, Brender JD, et al., 'Drinking water nitrate and human health: an updated review', *Int J Environ Res Public Health*, 2018, https://www.ncbi.nlm.nih.gov/pmc/articles/PMC6068531/

106 Oliver Millman, '"Dead zone" in Gulf of Mexico will take decades to recover from farm pollution', *The Guardian*, 2018, https://www.theguardian.com/environment/2018/mar/22/dead-zone-gulf-of-mexico-decades-recover-study

107 Environmental Working Group. 2021. *Do Farm Subsidies Fuel Farm Pollution?* [online] Available at: https://www.ewg.org/agmag/2016/04/do-farm-subsidies-fuel-farm-pollution

108 Matt Apuzzo, Selam Gebrekidan, Agustin Armendariz and Jin Wu, 2019. 'Killer slime, dead bids, an expunged map: The dirty secrets of European farm subsidies', Nytimes.com. [online] Available at: https://www.nytimes.com/interactive/2019/12/25/world/europe/farms-environment.html

109 Future Learn, 'Impact of climate change on agriculture', University of Reading, 2019, https://www.futurelearn.com/courses/climate-smart-agriculture/0/steps/26565

110 Report, 'Climate change adaptation in the agriculture sector in Europe', European Environmental Agency, 2019, https://www.euroseeds.eu/app/uploads/2019/09/Climate-change-adaptation-in-the-agriculture-sector-in-Europe.pdf

111 Ibid.

112 2019. *Special Report Climate Change and Land*. Food Security. [online] United Nations Intergovernmental Panel on Climate Change. Available at: https://www.ipcc.ch/srccl/

113 Fao.org. 2021. [online] Available at: http://www.fao.org/3/i4434e/i4434e.pdf

114 2009. *High Level Expert Forum*. 'How to feed the world 2050'. [online] Rome. Available at: http://www.fao.org/fileadmin/templates/wsfs/docs/Issues_papers/HLEF2050_Global_Agriculture.pdf

115 ScienceDaily. 2018. 'Record-wet and record-dry months increased in regions worldwide'. [online] Available at: https://www.sciencedaily.com/releases/2018/12/181212121857.htm

116 Grover-Kepec, E., Dilley, M., 'Documenting Drought-Related Disasters: A Global Reassessment', (2007), *The Journal of Environment & Development*, 2021. [online] Available at: https://www.researchgate.net/publication/249831241_Documenting_Drought-Related_DisastersA_Global_Reassessment

117 Reinl, J. (2019). *Desertification Costs World Economy up to $15 Trillion: UN*. [online] The Wire. Available at: https://thewire.in/environment/desertification-costs-world-economy-up-to-15-trillion-un

118 Ibid.

119 ABC News. 2019. 'More than a million flee as "extremely severe" Cyclone Fani hits Indian coast'. [online] Available at: https://www.abc.net.au/news/2019–05–03/india-mass-evacuation-ahead-of-cyclone/11076520

120 Report, 'FAO warns that recent torrential rains and cyclones could favour locust surge', FAO United Nations, 2015, http://www.fao.org/news/story/en/item/343656/icode/

121 Stone, M. (2020). 'A plague of locusts has descended on East Africa. Climate change may be to blame'. *National Geographic*.[online] 15 Feb. Available at: https://www.nationalgeographic.com/science/article/locust-plague-climate-science-east-africa

122 Cohen Gilliland, H. (2020). 'Gigantic new locust swarms hit East Africa', *National Geographic*. [online] 13 May. Available at: https://www.nationalgeographic.com/animals/article/gigantic-locust-swarms-hit-east-africa

123 World Bank. (n.d.). *The Locust Crisis: The World Bank's Response*. [online] Available at: https://www.worldbank.org/en/news/factsheet/2020/04/27/the-locust-crisis-the-world-banks-response

124 Forster, N. and Handelman, H. (1982). *Government Policy and Nutrition in Revolutionary Cuba: Rationing and Redistribution*. [online] UFSI. Available at: http://www.icwa.org/wp-content/uploads/2015/11/HH-13.pdf

125 Beverly Merz, 'Micronutrients have major impact on health', Harvard Medical School, 2016, https://www.health.harvard.edu/staying-healthy/micronutrients-have-major-impact-on-health

126 Micheal Schirber, 'The chemistry of life', *Livescience*, 2009, https://www.livescience.com/3505-chemistry-life-human-body.html

127 Plant-based diets centre on foods predominantly from plants. This includes not only fruits and vegetables, but also seeds, nuts, legumes, beans, whole grains and oils. It does not mean that you do not eat meat or dairy or that you are vegetarian or vegan. (health.harvard.edu)

128 Selhub, Eva MD, 2021. 'Nutritional psychiatry: Your brain on food'. [online] Harvard Health Blog. Available at: https://www.health.harvard.edu/blog/nutritional-psychiatry-your-brain-on-food-201511168626 [Accessed 2 May 2021]

129 Environmentalpollutioncenters.org. 2021. 'What is food pollution?'. [online] Available at: https://www.environmentalpollutioncenters.org/food/

130 Australian Institute of Food Safety. 2021. 'What are the different types of food contamination?'. [online] Available at: https://www.foodsafety.com.au/faq/what-are-the-different-types-of-food-contamination

131 Claire McCarthy, M., 2021. 'Common food additives and chemicals harmful to children'. [online] Harvard Health Blog. Available at: https://www.health.harvard.edu/blog/common-food-additives-and-chemicals-harmful-to-children-2018072414326

132 Springs Eternal. 2021. 'Unwanted health consequences of high-heat cooking'. [online] Available at: https://springseternal.com/unwanted-health-consequences-of-high-heat-cooking/

133 ResearchGate. 2021. 'Introduction to food process toxicants'. [online] Available at: https://www.researchgate.net/publication/229693483_Introduction_to_Food_Process_Toxicants

134 Livingston, M., 2021. 'How sugar can sabotage your immune system'. [online] CNET. Available at: https://www.cnet.com/health/nutrition/sugar-can-lower-your-immune-system/

135 *The Huffington Post*. 2021. 'Sugar is not only a drug but a poison too'. [online] Available at: https://www.huffpost.com/entry/sugar-is-not-only-a-drug-but-a-poison-too_b_8918630

136 Miller, V., Yusuf, S., Chow, C., Dehghan, M., Corsi, D., Lock, K., Popkin, B., Rangarajan, S., Khatib, R., Lear, S., Mony, P., Kaur, M., Mohan, V., Vijayakumar, K., Gupta, R., Kruger, A., Tsolekile, L., Mohammadifard, N., Rahman, O., Rosengren, A., Avezum, A., Orlandini, A., Ismail, N.,

Lopez-Jaramillo, P., Yusufali, A., Karsidag, K., Iqbal, R., Chifamba, J., Oakley, S., Ariffin, F., Zatonska, K., Poirier, P., Wei, L., Jian, B., Hui, C., Xu, L., Xiulin, B., Teo, K. and Mente, A., 2021. *Availability, affordability, and consumption of fruits and vegetables in 18 countries across income levels: findings from the Prospective Urban Rural Epidemiology (PURE) study*

137 Lindsay Horgan, 2018. 'Food demand in Australia: trends and issues 2018'. Available at: http://data.daff.gov.au/data/warehouse/9aat/2018/fdati9aat20180822/FoodDemandInAustralia_20180822_v1.0.0.pdf

138 Ibid.

139 Vetter, D., 2021. 'Guess which two countries produce the most plastic trash per person?'. [online] *Forbes*. Available at: https://www.forbes.com/sites/davidrvetter/2020/11/11/which-two-countries-produce-the-most-plastic-trash-per-person/

140 Phillip Callahan Ph.D., 1995. *Paramagnetism: Rediscovering Nature's Secret Force of Growth*, Acres, USA

141 Bruce Ames, 'Dietary Pesticides', National Academy of Sciences, 1990, https://www.pnas.org/content/pnas/87/19/7777.full.pdf

142 Abdul Rashid War, Hari Chand Sharma, Michael Gabriel Paulraj, Mohd Yousf War & Savarimuthu Ignacimuthu, 2021. 'Herbivore induced plant volatiles: Their role in plant defense for pest management'. [online] Available at: https://www.researchgate.net/publication

143 NationofChange. 2021. *Monsanto wins $7.7b lawsuit in Brazil – but farmers' fight to stop its 'amoral' royalty system will continue – NationofChange*. [online] Available at: https://www.nationofchange.org/2019/11/02/monsanto-wins-7–7b-lawsuit-in-brazil-but-farmers-fight-to-stop-its-amoral-royalty-system-will-continue/

144 Ibid.

145 J. Edward Moreno, 'Nearly 30 million Americans reported not having enough food to eat last week', The Hill News Service, 2020, https://thehill.com/homenews/news/509749-nearly-30-million-americans-reported-food-insecurity-last-week-census-data

146 Larry Elliott, 'Low wages are "return to pre-industrial Britain", says Bank of England economist', *The Guardian*, 2021. [online] Available at: https://www.theguardian.com/business/2017/jun/21/slow-wage-growth-down-to-return-to-the-past-bank-of-england-chief-economist

147 Caitlin Dewey, 'Why farmers are getting less and less of every dollar Americans spend on food', *The Washington Post*, 2018. Retrieved

9 March 2022, from https://www.washingtonpost.com/news/wonk/wp/2018/05/02/why-farmers-only-get-7-8-cents-of-every-dollar-americans-spend-on-food/

148 Iwatani, S. and Yamamoto, N., 2021. 'Functional food products in Japan: a review'. Available at: https://www.semanticscholar.org/paper/Functional-food-products-in-Japan%3A-A-review-Iwatani-Yamamoto/bdec3614bf125ebc3554f760a3582b3300c09147

149 Leonhardt, M., 'Americans now spend twice as much on health care as they did in the 1980s'. 2019. *CNBC.* [online] Available at: https://www.cnbc.com/2019/10/09/americans-spend-twice-as-much-on-health-care-today-as-in-the-1980s.html [Accessed 29 April 2021].

150 2021. [online] Available at: https://www.researchgate.net/publication/317914442_Assessing_the_economic_costs_of_unhealthy_diets_and_low_physical_activity_An_evidence_review_and_proposed_framework

151 Sawicki, N., Lichtblau, M., Johnson, G. and Moclair, K., 2021. 'The price of eating right'. [online] *Brown Political Review.* Available at: https://brownpoliticalreview.org/2021/03/the-price-of-eating-right/

152 Swaminathan, R., 'Magnesium metabolism and its disorders.' *The Clinical Biochemist.* Reviews vol. 24,2 (2003): 47–66.

153 Kansas State University, 'Gardening gives older adults benefits like hand strength and self esteem', *ScienceDaily*, www.sciencedaily.com/releases/2009/02/090203142517

154 mindbodygreen. 2021. 'The research is in: Yes, gardening totally counts as exercise'. [online] Available at: https://www.mindbodygreen.com/0–18323/9-reasons-gardening-is-the-ultimate-mindbody-workout.html

155 Alexandra Topping, 'Gardening as good as exercise in cutting heart attack risk, study shows', *The Guardian*, 2013. https://www.theguardian.com/society/2013/oct/28/gardening-exercise-cutting-heart-attack-risk-diy-60-plus

156 Thompson, R., 2018. 'Gardening for health: a regular dose of gardening', *Clin Med* (London). June; 18(3): 201–205.

157 ScienceDaily.com, 2022 [online]. 'Healthy, stress-busting fat found hidden in dirt', https://www.sciencedaily.com/releases/2019/05/190529094003.htm [Accessed 30 April 2022.]

158 Un.org. 2021. [online] Available at: https://www.un.org/en/development/desa/population/publications/pdf/ageing/WorldPopulationAgeing2019-Highlights.pdf

159 Dr Claire Morris, 'Nutrients and bioactives in green leafy vegetables and cognitive decline', National Institute of Aging, 2018, https://www.nia.nih.gov/news/leafy-greens-linked-slower-age-related-cognitive-decline

160 Ritchie, H. and Roser, M., 2021. *Meat and Dairy Production.* [online] Our World in Data. Available at: https://ourworldindata.org/meat-production

161 Crowe, T., 2021. 'What we can learn from the world's longest-lived people'. [online] Thinking Nutrition. Available at: https://www.thinkingnutrition.com.au/lifestyles-long-lived-people/

162 Dpi.nsw.gov.au. 2021. *Protected cropping.* [online] Available at: https://www.dpi.nsw.gov.au/agriculture/horticulture/greenhouse

163 Harvard Health. 2022. 'Add color to your diet for good nutrition'. [online] Available at: https://www.health.harvard.edu/staying-healthy/add-color-to-your-diet-for-good-nutrition

164 S.H. Wittwer, F.G. Teubner, 'Foliar Absorption of Mineral Nutrients', *Annual Review of Plant Physiology*, Vol. 10:13-30 (Volume publication date June 1959). Available at: https://doi.org/10.1146/annurev.pp.10.060159.000305

INDEX

G